Book of the American Indians

BROWN PAPER SCHOOL
USKids History: Book of the American Indians

Written by Marlene Smith-Baranzini *and* Howard Egger-Bovet

Illustrated by T. Taylor Bruce

James J. Rawls, *Consulting Editor*

Little, Brown and Company
Boston   New York   Toronto   London

A Yolla Bolly Press Book

USKids History: Book of the American Indians was edited and prepared for publication at The Yolla Bolly Press, Covelo, California. The series is under the supervision of James Robertson and Carolyn Robertson. Production staff: Diana Fairbanks, Renée Menge, and Alexandra Chappell. Composition by Wilsted & Taylor, Oakland, California.

Acknowledgments

The authors would like to thank Terry P. Wilson, Chairman of the Native American Studies Department at the University of California at Berkeley, for his consultation and review of the material used in this book.

The authors also thank William Broder for the loan of visual and other material from his collection. Acknowledgment is given to the following for permission to reprint photographs: Lowie Museum of Anthropology, University of California, Berkeley: p. 20; Milwaukee Public Museum: p. 10; Museum of Northern Arizona: p. 43 left (photo by Mark Middleton), middle (photo by Marc Gaede), right (Marc Gaede); National Anthropological Archives, Smithsonian Institution: p. 46, 64, 67; Phoebe Hearst Museum of Anthropology, University of California at Berkeley: p. 25.

Acknowledgment is given to the following for permission to reprint material originally published elsewhere. *Indian Legends from the Northern Rockies*, © 1966, by Ella Clark, University of Oklahoma Press; *Indian Legends of the Pacific Northwest*, by Ella Clark, © 1981, University of California Press; *Meditations with Animals*, by Gerald Hausman, © 1986, Bear & Co. Inc.; *The Northern Maidu*, by Marie Potts, © 1977, Naturegraph Publishers; *Sun Chief*, Simmons (ed.), © 1942, Yale University Press.

FIRST EDITION

ISBN: 0-316-96921-4 (hc)
ISBN: 0-316-22208-9 (pb)
HC: 10 9 8 7 6 5 4 3 2 1
PB: 10 9 8 7 6 5 4 3 2 1

MV-NY

Published simultaneously in Canada by Little, Brown & Company (Canada) Limited

Printed in the United States of America

Library of Congress Cataloging-in-Publication Data

Smith-Baranzini, Marlene.
    Book of the American Indians / written by Marlene Smith-Baranzini and Howard Egger-Bovet ; illustrated by T. Taylor Bruce. — 1st ed.
        p.   cm. — (USKids history)
    Summary: Offers insights into the day-to-day lives, customs, and beliefs of various North American Indian tribes before the arrival of the Europeans. Includes ideas for related activities.
    ISBN 0-316-96921-4 (hc)
    ISBN 0-316-22208-9 (pb)
    1. Indians of North America—Juvenile literature.   [1. Indians of North America.]   I. Egger-Bovet, Howard.   II. Bruce, T. Taylor, ill.   III. Title.   IV. Series.
E77.4.E44   1994
970.004'97—dc20   93-3068

Contents

Note: Activities and games are italicized.

People of the Northwest

How Raven Helped the Ancient People

When his bill began to burn, he dropped the firebrand.

Long ago, near the beginning of the world, Gray Eagle was the guardian of the sun and moon and stars, of fresh water and of fire. Gray Eagle hated people so much that he kept these things hidden. People lived in darkness, without fire and without water.

Gray Eagle had a beautiful daughter, and Raven fell in love with her. At that time Raven was a handsome young man. He changed himself into a snow-white bird, and as a snow-white bird, he pleased Gray Eagle's daughter. She invited him to her father's lodge.

When Raven saw the sun and the moon and the stars and fresh water hanging on the sides of Eagle's lodge, he knew what he should do. He watched for his chance to seize them when no one was looking. He stole all of them, and a brand of fire also, and flew out of the lodge through the smoke hole.

As soon as Raven got outside, he hung the sun up in the sky. It made so much light that he was able to fly far out to an island in the middle of the ocean. When the sun set, he fastened the moon up in the sky and hung the stars around in different places. By this new light he kept on flying, carrying with him the fresh water and the brand of fire he had stolen. He flew back over the land. When he had reached the right place, he dropped all the water he had stolen. It fell to the ground, and there it became the source of all the fresh-water streams and lakes in the world.

Then Raven flew on, holding the brand of fire in his bill. The smoke from the fire flew back over his white feathers and made them black. When his bill began to burn, he had to drop the firebrand. It struck rocks and went into them. That is why, if you strike two stones together, fire will drop out.

Raven's feathers never became white again after they were blackened by the smoke from the firebrand. That is why Raven is now a black bird. *(A Northwest Indian Myth)*

A WALK ACROSS THE ANCIENT WORLD

The very first people came to North America so long ago that it's hard to imagine such a time. The evidence they left tells us this land was settled more than 25,000 years ago, and probably much earlier. We don't know everything about those who lived here first, but they left some valuable clues that help us imagine their lives.

For one thing, one of the early people made a ten-inch scraper from the leg bone of a caribou. Whoever made it put a row of notches, little V-shaped cuts, in the wide end of the bone. The scraper might have been used to clean animal skins before making them into clothing or blankets. It was found in Yukon Territory, in northern Canada.

A scientific test that is called radiocarbon dating, C*14* for short, was used to test the age of this bone scraper. Archaeologists think the scraper is about 27,000 years old. That makes it the oldest human-made object found in North America.

Scientists think other clues about the earliest people in North America lie hidden in Siberia or Alaska, or under the Bering Sea. Why? Because they believe this is the area where people first came to North America.

To see how people probably got here, and where they came from, look on a map. Find North America, then go north until you find the North Pole. Put your finger on it. Now move your finger down and to the left, or west, and find the place where two continents, Asia and North America, are separated by a narrow strip of water. That water is the Bering Strait. It's only fifty-six miles wide. On a clear day if you stand on one side, you can see across to the other.

Mountains of Ice Covered It Twice

At least twice in the history of the earth, mountains of ice—glaciers—covered this area of the world. During the ice ages, the level of the ocean dropped. As it fell, water drained from the Bering Strait and left it a dry strip of land. In that one narrow place, Alaska and Siberia were joined together.

When we refer to the Bering Strait during the two ice ages, we call it Beringia. People from Asia could have walked across Beringia into North America then, and they probably did. (In fact, they probably wandered back and forth a bit. They might have started from North America and walked east to Asia, or crossed the water in boats, as other scientists believe.)

The first ice age occurred between 36,000 and 32,000 years ago. The second occurred between 28,000 and 13,000 years ago. Toward the end of the first ice age, the glaciers melted back and left the land wide open. People could have followed the animal herds they hunted, down into Alaska and Canada.

As the ice age ended, the weather warmed, the glaciers melted back more, their water ran into the ocean again, filling it higher. For thousands of years, Asia and North America were again separated by water.

Two Ways of Knowing

Indian stories like "How Raven Helped the Ancient People" are called creation accounts. They explain how the world began and how all beings once lived together.

Every tribe has different accounts, but often the stories are similar. They were told over and over, and everyone in the tribe knew them well. Little has changed in them for hundreds of years. They are the heart of Indian tribal literature.

Like Indian accounts, scientific evidence also helps explain our world. Scientists who study ancient civilizations are called archaeologists. They work with anthropologists, who study how people have changed from long ago times. They search for clues that show where people have lived and how they got there. Their findings are another way of discovering the mysteries of life.

Ancient accounts and recent evidence are two ways of knowing. Both ways teach us important ideas about the world.

People may have followed the animal herds they hunted.

Make a Bullroarer

Young boys of the Pacific Northwest Coast tribes made a toy that had a special purpose. Its Indian name is not known, but today it is called a bullroarer. In the Northwest, boys used it to call the rain. Because it sounded like the wind, too, Indian tribes of the plains also held it sacred.

You can make a bullroarer. Whirling it will bring the voice of the wind.

You Will Need:

A flat piece of softwood, such as pine, ½ inch thick, about 3 inches wide, and about a foot long; a yard of strong twine; a pocketknife, drill, sandpaper, and paint.

Whittle the corners of the wood to round. Look at the illustration and see how the top surface is whittled from the center to the sides, giving the top of the bullroarer a convex shape. (The slope allows the wind to flow easily over the surface of the bullroarer.) Ask a grownup to help you drill a hole for the twine in the center of one end. Sand the bullroarer.

Decorate the bullroarer with a thunderbird or lightning design, or create a weather design of your own. Tie the twine through the hole and give it a firm knot.

Be sure you only whirl your bullroarer in an open space where it won't hit anyone or anything.

Acoma Design

During the second ice age, the glacier again pulled water from the ocean, the way a sponge soaks up spilled milk. The continents joined again. But if people tried to cross Beringia between 28,000 and 13,000 years ago, they could not have gone very far into North America. A glacier still covered Alaska and Canada. In some places the frozen wall stood one mile high. It would have stopped them.

Not Your Average Summer Hike

The evidence that shows Bering Strait and Beringia, sometimes water and sometimes land—and the glaciers, sometimes huge and sometimes melted back—gives scientists a pretty good idea about when the first people were able to walk from Asia and migrate south into the unexplored lands of North America. They probably came between 36,000 and 32,000 years ago, during the first ice age, when Beringia was dry but the Alaska glacier wall did not block their way south. How long did it take them to come here? The journey into this new world took many lifetimes. In the beginning, perhaps only a small band of thirty or more people crossed Beringia. They probably made camps on the tundra, and they stayed there during the darkest and coldest part of the year. Bone and stone scrapers and choppers found in Texas, very similar to the caribou scraper found in the Yukon, tell us that early people were strong and fit and *did* eventually travel far into North America.

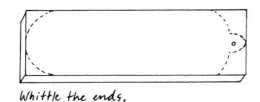

Whittle the ends.

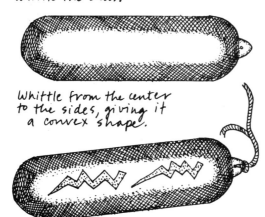

Whittle from the center to the sides, giving it a convex shape.

Drill a hole, sand, and decorate.

THE SPIRIT OF THE STORM

Rain. It fell hard, soaking the earth. In winter, the wind howled, driving the rain wildly. In spring, summer, and autumn, too, rain poured steadily down from the sky. Fog rolled in from the seacoast. It misted the air and hid the dark trees that covered the hills.

Above the peaks of the tallest mountains, a huge bird lived in the clouds. Its wings flapped and made thunder. Its eyes flashed and made lightning. Its name was Thunderbird, the spirit of the storm.

When Thunderbird was hungry, it swooped down along the Pacific Ocean and got whales for its food. As it flew home to the top of the mountain, clouds, thunder, and rain often followed it. No one had ever seen Thunderbird. Yet they all feared its power. The people knew that terrible storms would come if Thunderbird was angry. They tried to live so that Thunderbird would be pleased with them.

Some of the people believed that before they came, the animal kingdom had ruled the earth. Others believed that they had always lived here. Yet the tribes were alike in many ways. The rain brought things that made life easy for them. In the spring, they dug the tender bulbs of lilies that bloomed in the fields and marshes. In summer, they picked juicy blackberries, raspberries, and salmonberries that grew in thick tangles in the meadows. They hunted quail and dove, deer and small animals. From the rivers, they caught many kinds of fish. They ate bass, trout, and salmon. The people had an abundance of food. But the salmon was the heart of their diet.

They depended on salmon for their survival.

CELEBRATING THE SALMON

From its source high in the mountains, the Quinault River flows steadily toward the ocean. Long ago, Indians settled in villages along the river. Those in the largest village called themselves *kwin'ail*. That is how the river, too, came to be named the Quinault (KWIN-alt). The Indians fished its freezing waters for the salmon, their source of life.

The Quinault depended on salmon for their survival. Each year, to ensure that they would receive an abundant catch, as their ancestors always had, the Indians honored the salmon run, the catch, and the feast. They did not take the fish carelessly or quickly. Its life was as important to them as their own lives were. Eating the salmon meat, they believed, joined them flesh to flesh with this life-giving food. Rituals and ceremonies accompanied every act of killing, roasting, and eating the salmon, and disposing of the unused flesh and bones.

Late in the winter, the salmon run began. As the idle, dark days of winter grew longer and lighter, the Quinault prepared for the first catch. Five species of this fish lived—and live now—in the Northwest.

But for the Quinault, salmon were much more than fish caught in rivers. All the tribes on the Northwest Coast, in fact, believed the salmon held great power. According to Quinault belief, the salmon lived under the ocean in wonderful houses, where they took human forms. They knew that the Indians depended on them for food. So each year during the salmon run, the fish sacrificed themselves to be caught and eaten. After they had died, their spirits returned to the ocean and became human-like again.

The people showed their respect by treating the salmon with the utmost honor. With the first catch from the river each year, they held a ceremony to celebrate the salmon run. They called it First Salmon. It was followed by a feast that lasted several days.

King of the River

Five species of salmon are native to the Pacific Northwest. To make it confusing, each species is known by two or more names. The largest of the five species is the king or chinook. The others are the coho or silver, red or sockeye, humpback or pink, and chum or dog.

From their birthplace in the river, they swim downstream toward the ocean. They spend their adult lives in saltwater.

At spawning, or egg-laying time, the salmon return to freshwater rivers like the Quinault, to the very place where they were born. If the river bottom has been undisturbed, a salmon will find the very patch of gravel it hatched on, and lay its eggs.

After their eggs have been laid, the old salmon die. The young hatch and swim to the ocean.

Black Salmon's First Vision

Naked, Black Salmon plunged into the gray water.

Guardian Spirits and Medicine Power

This is an old teaching: Every living thing is watched over by a guardian spirit. The Quinault and other people in the Pacific Northwest, and most Native Americans everywhere, know this. They use prayers, ceremonies, and rituals to please the guardian spirits so they will want to help. Whalers spoke to the whale spirit so it would not be upset at their hunting. Even the harpoon was treated with respect, or it would not work well in the hunt.

When a boy was about to become a man, he would try to find his own guardian spirit. He followed strict rules of behavior. He would not eat for several days, and at night he would go off by himself. He might go alone to the ocean, where many spirits lived. He waited for some sign that would tell him what kind of special power he would receive.

(This account of a Quinault boy's vision quest is based on real experiences reported many years ago.)

Black Salmon (Ka'mkan) opened his eyes to the sound of his father's voice.

"Wake up and go bathe before the water wakes up. It is not as cold now as it will be when it wakes up," his father said. Black Salmon shoved his cedar blanket aside and rose to his feet. No one else in his family was yet awake. He left the dark house and headed toward the river. His breath made clouds in the cold air.

Naked, Black Salmon plunged into the gray water. An icy jolt shot through his body. He waded back to shore, to the bank where he kept a braid of vine maple. He scrubbed his body with the bough until his skin burned. Then he dashed into the water again. He repeated this ritual four times, and then he went home.

Black Salmon was fourteen. He had bathed in the Quinault River every morning for five years. In the dead of winter, small stones sometimes stuck to his feet as he walked home, and on humid summer days, clouds of gnats swarmed around his face. But he came to the river daily. He believed that if a raven pecked his eyes blind, he could still find his way.

Black Salmon might have one guardian spirit or many, but the first one was often the most potent. Some spirits helped a man have great wealth. Others assured him power to heal the sick or to win at gambling or in war. Black Salmon wanted to possess the skill of a great hunter.

One day Black Salmon and his father were working beside several men in the village, trimming hemlock poles for a new weir, an enclosure set in water to catch fish. They stood the frame of poles across the river, with wide nets lashed to it that would trap fish. Everyone worked together; the women wove the baskets, and the men gathered and trimmed the poles and placed the weirs at intervals in the river.

Black Salmon's father set down his abalone knife and looked at his son. Black Salmon guessed at once what the elder was about to say.

"Black Salmon, you are ready to leave. Tomorrow, before the day breaks, choose your way and go. You will be alone, but I will say prayers for you. You will know when it is time to return."

The boy nodded but said nothing. He had spent years preparing for this day, and now he felt both bright and dark. He continued peeling bark from his pole, often glancing toward the northeast, to the direction he had already decided he would go.

Black Salmon said good-bye to his family that night. In the morning, he took three dried blackberry cakes and went to the river as he always did. As he left the village, hunger began to gnaw inside him. He had far to go.

The land beyond the village was flat and thick with cedar, hemlock, and fir trees that hid the horizon. Black Salmon could not yet see the mountain. Many miles ahead, the river narrowed to its source, a small, swift creek tumbling out of the mountain. It would take him two days, maybe more, to reach the mountain. At night he wouldn't sleep. He would stay close to the water so he would not lose his way. He stopped twice for a drink, scooping the cold water into his cupped hand. Once he jumped in to bathe. His thoughts seemed sharper after that.

All night Black Salmon walked, breaking off a bit of berry cake to chew now and then. The next day he followed the river, too, going behind villages so he would not be tempted to talk to anyone. In the afternoon, the land began to grow hilly. Black Salmon pushed his way through tangles of blackberries. He climbed slowly now, waiting for a feeling to guide him in the direction he should go.

Finally, Black Salmon stopped walking. He had come to a flat spot on the side of the mountain. To the west, he could see the ocean. Along the river below, threads of smoke rose from the villages. He, too, built a fire, and sat down beside it.

The night grew cold. Black Salmon looked up to the sky and prayed, "I want you to help me." He did not know how long he had been sitting, or when his guardian spirit might come. It might take several days, weeks, or even years. The spirit would bring him a vision—an experience between reality and dreaming, but with lasting power.

While Black Salmon was praying, he felt the wind rise. It began to howl, rushing in all directions. Branches snapped and crashed from the trees. The ground began to shake, and somewhere close, an eagle screamed. Black Salmon thought of running away. Snake appeared before him and then disappeared. Then Thunderbird flew down. Black Salmon thought he would be carried into the sky. Instead, Thunderbird changed into a human form and danced around the fire. The sky flashed. Suddenly Thunderbird vanished.

Black Salmon stayed on the mountain for two days. He could not eat. Most of the time, he slept. His guardian spirit came to him in a vision and talked to him. He told Black Salmon to make a Thunderbird rattle. He taught the boy songs and showed him dances to be performed when he went back to the village. He told Black Salmon things he must never repeat. Black Salmon knew the power had come to him. He would go home.

He felt the wind rise. It began to howl.

The Whale Hunters

They paddled close enough to throw the harpoon.

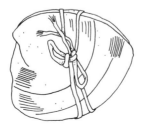

When going whale hunting, the Makah packed coals inside two clamshells and tied them together. This prevented the coals from getting wet or hopping out into the canoe.

"My dad used to pray and prepare himself for months ahead of whaling season," the Indian man said. "He knew special songs to bring power, and he had magic amulets and charms that he kept in a secret place and wouldn't let the rest of us see."

In the Makah village on the coast, his father had been one of the most honored men. Very few received power from whale spirits. Such men were chosen to hunt the great whale. His father was their leader.

The hunters would be guided by the whale spirits. They wanted everything to be correct when the huge mammal appeared. Its flesh would feed their village for months, and they de-

pended on its thick fat—blubber—to make oil for eating and cooking. From its bones they could carve many tools. But the whalers would not paddle out to hunt whales until the entire village was ready.

Each member of the Makah village had things to do to prepare for the whale hunt. Usually sixteen men hunted whales together, eight in each canoe. Every hunter had baskets to mend and harpoons to make or sharpen. Just as important as the sharp harpoons that would pierce the whale's back were the coils of red cedar rope they placed neatly inside the baskets.

The Makah tied sealskin floats to the long ropes. Every harpoon was also attached to a rope. When the harpoon sailed over the water and into the whale's side, the rope flew out of the basket with it. Like thick, dark balloons, the floats kept the rope on the surface of the water. They slowed the whale as it dived. Watching the floats and baskets tied to the ropes, the Makah knew exactly where the whale went. Eventually, the whale would tire and come to rest on the surface.

The men gathered everything they would need, and carefully packed their canoes. They had no idea how long the hunt might last. They were careful to prepare extra food. They took dried fish, oil, and drinking water, which they carried in sealskin bags. The weather could change quickly. But the men even planned for that. They took everything they would need to build a warm fire.

But how could they light a fire in a canoe on the ocean? The Makah, like nearly all the tribes of the Pacific Northwest, kept a small fire burning in every home. In such a damp and rainy climate, they could never count on finding dry firewood. It made more sense to keep a small fire going all the time. So on the hunt they carried hot coals from such a fire. They packed the coals carefully inside two clamshells and tied them tightly together. That kept them from getting wet or going out. When the whalers needed fire, the clamshells could be opened and set inside a wooden box with sand on the bottom. By adding some wood, they would soon have a small fire.

When everything was packed into the canoes, the men had one more responsibility before they could leave. They would say a final prayer that the whale would come to them. The leader of the hunt, too, had one more special duty.

Singing, the hunters paddled home.

"My dad would swim out around the rocks beyond the surf, diving and spouting like a whale. He was pretending to be a whale to show that his heart was right. A man needed all the spirit power he could get when he led his crew on a hunt."

Ready at last, the Makah men climbed into their canoes. In their homes in the village, their wives and children thought about them. All day long, working at their tasks, mothers would not shout, children would not run and yell. They believed their own loud actions could drive the harpooned whale deeper out into the ocean. Everyone knew that whales enjoyed coming to a quiet, orderly village.

Today the men were fortunate. In the gray distance ahead, a whale's massive body surfaced. Quietly, they paddled close enough to throw the harpoon. As the first hook hit the animal, the Indian who aimed it prayed again to the animal's spirit.

"Our people will come to welcome you," the man promised the whale's spirit. "Swim to our beach, and we will sing and dance for you. We will honor you. We will decorate you with fine feathers."

As each whaler in the first canoe thrust his harpoon point into the huge animal, the prayers were repeated. The ropes attached to the long spears uncoiled rapidly from the baskets and flew overboard into the icy water. The sealskin floats kept them on the surface.

Bright swirls of red blood from the whale's injuries filled the water. But the men did not grab the ropes and chase the whale. That would have been foolish and dangerous. One flip of the enormous tail could kill every man at once. Instead, they let the baskets and ropes show them the whale's trail.

When the whale grew tired, the Makah whalers paddled closer. But they still did not harpoon it to death. When it lay exhausted on the surface, one diver went overboard. He swam close. Aiming his spear, he sent the final blow into the whale's heart. The huge whale lay still.

The hunt was victorious, but the hard work was not finished. The whale's mouth was laced shut so it would not fill with water and become impossibly heavy to drag home. Then the men pierced the whale's sides. They tied the floats to its skin, making it easier to pull through the water. Towing it behind their canoes took great strength.

At last the exhausted men turned their boats toward land. Smoke from their village fires rose in the misty air. Singing traditional songs of the whale hunt, the Makah whale hunters paddled proudly home.

A Day in the Village

It is time to get up.

Pale gray light fills the sky. It is time to get up. Your little sister, curled beside you on a mattress of marsh grass, is sleeping soundly. Good. You toss the heavy wolfskin blanket over her face as your toes touch the cool dirt floor. Your mother is already stirring the fire in a corner of the long room. She has opened the smoke hole in the roof.

Choosing two small logs from the woodpile stacked beneath the sleeping ledge, you carefully set them on the coals. Starting the fire burning again in the morning is your favorite job, but your sister usually beats you to it. You poke the hot coals and push the logs with your stick carefully, trying not to send sparks rising. On a drying rack hooked high above the fire, salmon hang in long rows. Outside, rain drizzles, but the warmth from the rising flames feels good.

You hear voices. Your father, older brother, and uncle have returned from their morning plunge in the river. You open the oval plank door for them. The minute your uncle spots you, he shakes his wet head, laughing as you run for cover. The men wrap up in cedar bark blankets to get warm.

Breakfast is ready. Your mother scoops it from a cedar cooking box beside the fire. Everyone sits cross-legged on the ledge against the wall, eating a thick stew of dried clams, fish oil, and camas bulbs. Your father is talking about the work ahead. He and your uncle, your brother, and other men in the village are going hunting.

After the food is put away and the house straightened, your mother and aunt will gather cattails to line the inside walls of the house. They will also start stripping bark from cedar trees, to make clothes. They need your help. Summers are usually cool and wet where you live, but the season of heavy rains is coming soon. Your family wears little clothing, and you often wear nothing at all. But everyone needs hats and wraps for winter rainstorms. Even the house will be warmer with an extra layer of reeds on the inside walls.

Walking to the marsh near the river, your aunt carries her baby boy on a cradleboard. It looks heavy, strapped to her back, but she doesn't complain. Your mother and aunt cut thick bunches of cattails. Many have their fuzzy brown seed heads on them. You and your sister run back and forth, piling them up to take home.

In the village, nearly everyone is outside at work. The hunters have not returned, but some men are carving designs in boxes and another group near the chief's longhouse is mending salmon nets. Two of the men are slaves who were captured by the chief on a warring party. Your family has no slaves, but many people in the village do. If your father captured prisoners from another tribe, he says he would need a larger house. Everyone in the village would help build it, but you like your house just as it is.

The afternoon sun is shining through a narrow slit in the clouds, and groups of women are taking their children to the ocean. You and your sister are going too. Your aunt unstraps the baby from the cradleboard so you can take him with you. He doesn't know how to walk yet, but he's good at sitting in the sand and putting things in his mouth. It's your job to make sure he only plays with clamshells or sticks that he can't choke on. If he gets hungry and cries, you will have to bring him home to his mother.

But at the beach, the baby falls fast asleep. The waves roar onto the shore. Seagulls swoop down among the rocks, crying out to each other. While the women dig clams, you and the six other children run along the beach, finding dead fish and huge tangles of kelp that have washed ashore.

It's hard work untwisting the long green kelp ropes, but finally they're separated. The longest one is more than seventeen feet from the fat root bulb to the tip. You choose teams. Each team grabs one end of the kelp rope and lines up with the tallest children first.

Digging your heels in the sand, you pull hard against your sister's team, but it's almost an even match. You pull with all your might. You begin to feel the other team weakening. All arms straining, your team jerks hard on the kelp. You are overpowering the enemy, backing up slowly as you drag them toward you. You are about to win, when suddenly, two of the enemy players drop the kelp. Screaming and laughing, your team flies backward, falling into a heap of heads, elbows, and knees in the sand. You are the winners!

Each team grabs one end of the kelp rope.

northwest
cedar

From Cedar Bark to Rainhats

Making trees into "cloth" might sound impossible to you, but for the women of the Northwest, it was ordinary work. Cedar grew in abundance in the lush forests. Indian women figured out a remarkable way of peeling, pounding, softening, and separating the bark so the fibers could be woven into sturdy coverings. Cedar blankets were highly prized among the people, and cedar clothing was more common than garments made of leather.

But clothing was not important to the people. When it rained, men often kept dry under wide cedar hats and cedar "raincoats." Women usually wore cedar bark skirts or aprons. The children often wore nothing at all. But when it was cold, everyone wrapped up in animal furs or cedar blankets to stay warm.

cedar chest

cedar ceremonial mask

men's cedar bark raincoat

cedar bark hats

cedar bark skirt

Players on the opposite team try to make the walker laugh.

STICK IN THE SAND

Quinault children did not spend every minute of the day helping their parents. Like all children, they thought up games to play together.

At the beach, girls played a team game that called for true willpower. First, each team made a sculpture of a face in the sand, with shells and pebbles to mark the eyes and mouth. When the sculpture was finished, they stuck a long stick into the sand in front of it. Then the real challenge began. Players took turns trying to walk to the other team's sculpture and to get the stick without smiling or laughing. Players on the opposite team did everything they could think of to make the girl laugh and lose her turn.

In this faster version of the game, you don't make a sand sculpture. You can play anyplace where two sticks can be pushed into the ground so they stand up.

You Will Need:

A strip of beach, lawn, or field; two long sticks or poles; and any number of friends.

Decide how far apart the sticks should be, then push them firmly into the ground. Divide into two teams. (If you have an odd number of players, let one person on the smaller team take two turns.)

A player on the first team calls out to someone on the other team to come and get the stick. The player on the opposite team walks across to the other team's stick and gets it *without smiling or laughing.*

Players on the opposite team try to make the walker laugh. They may shout, make faces, or tell jokes. When the player who is walking toward the stick begins to smile or laugh, his or her turn is over. The player returns to his or her team's stick and calls a player on the other team to come over and get the stick.

When a player touches the stick without smiling, he or she earns one point. But every time a player laughs or smiles, the other team takes its turn. When all players have been called, the game is over. The team with the most points is the winner.

Raspberries and Honey

After the long work of preparing and drying fish and meat for winter, the women turned to gathering fresh berries. Wild blackberries, blueberries, raspberries, and cranberries tasted wonderful.

Berrypicking was a happy time. The younger girls watched the children and babies. Sometimes women from several villages gathered together, camping in the countryside for several days. As they picked berries, they caught up on village news.

"Indian ice cream" was one of their treats. The women made it by beating dried berries with fish oil and snow. You might like making this simple dessert instead.

1 quart fresh
  raspberries*
½ cup honey

In a blender or food processor, puree berries with honey until smooth. Chill well and serve.

Makes 4 to 6 servings.

* You can substitute strawberries, blueberries, or blackberries for the fruit.

The Potlatch Celebration

A long procession of canoes arrived from every direction.

These two masks were used in ceremonies by Northwest Coast Indians. The one above is the face of a person, and the one below is the face of a wolf.

Winter was the quietest season for the Quinault. But it was still a busy time. The chief usually invited acquaintances from near and far to an elaborate celebration. Perhaps his son had received a vision naming his power. This would mean he would get a new name. The gathering that marked such important events was called a potlatch. It often lasted several days, and sometimes took many months to plan.

When a chief decided to have a potlatch, he counted his possessions—his canoes, his blankets, his dentalium (shell money), and everything else he owned. He called a tallyman to help him keep track of how many gifts he could give to each guest. If he did not think he had enough property for everyone, he asked family members to help him make extra things. At the potlatch he would give away nearly everything he owned. He often built a huge, new longhouse with enough room for everyone.

Then the chief announced his potlatch. Messengers went by canoe from village to village to make formal invitations to the guests. Even the dogs were invited! Guests who accepted the invitation sent money or blankets back to the chief. They, too, liked to show how prosperous they were.

On the day the potlatch began, a long procession of canoes arrived from every direction. Families paddled up to the village, parading back and forth in their canoes, singing songs. When they came to greet the chief, they received gifts of welcome.

On the first afternoon everyone played games and tried their skill at wrestling or foot racing. They gambled over who would be the strongest or fastest. Late in the afternoon each tribe gathered to paint their faces and put on costumes for the evening ceremonial dance. As visitors, they were expected to entertain the chief and his villagers. The audience would argue over who were the best performers.

During the potlatch, the chief made certain that everyone was continuously fed. He would be humiliated if he ran short of anything. Guests, too, ate as much as they could, so as not to seem rude.

On the last day, the chief's final gifts to everyone were piled high on a blanket spread on the floor of the longhouse. The crowd lined up around the walls of the room, waiting to see what they would get. Each person was called forward, beginning with the most important, who received the very finest gifts. No one, however, went away empty-handed.

Once in a while it happened that villagers gave the chief more expensive gifts when they accepted the potlatch invitation than those they received in return. This was rare, but if the guests did not think their gifts were good enough, they might drag their gifts across the floor instead of carrying them.

When the blanket was finally empty, the chief held it up. Because it would be rude to leave him holding the blanket, a visiting chief came forward and took it from him. This signalled that the chief who took the blanket would give the next potlatch.

MAKE YOUR OWN DRUM

A clean round five-gallon ice cream tub (or a small metal wastebasket) is a good size for a drum. Covered with rawhide—untreated leather that dries stiff—it makes the deep drum song you're familiar with. You can beat it using your hands or drumsticks.

You Will Need:

A five-gallon cardboard ice cream tub (if you call an ice cream parlor, the manager may save one for you) or a round metal wastebasket; a piece of rawhide (sold in leather shops) that fits over the drum and extends an extra 2 inches down around the sides; strong twine to tie the rawhide (drumskin) onto the drum; and (optional) two 15-inch-long, ½-inch in diameter wood dowels for drumsticks.

1. Start with a clean container. If you want to decorate the outside, called the *drumshell*, do it before you put the drumskin on it. You can finish it with tribal designs drawn with permanent markers, or you can create symbols that represent things in your life. Or you could cover it with shelf-liner paper that looks like wood.

2. Measure the diameter of the drumbase and add 2 extra inches. (A 14-inch square of rawhide will cover the ice cream tub.) Cut the rawhide to size.

3. Soak the rawhide for about two hours in water to soften it. (Do it outside or in a well-ventilated area because it smells!) When it is soft, blot the rawhide between two towels or hang it up, to get rid of most of the water.

4. Cover the drumbase with the damp rawhide. Pull it gently toward the sides, so the top is smooth. Smooth the sides too—dry rawhide is stiff and tough.

5. Wrap several lengths of twine about an inch below the base of the drumskin to hold the rawhide in place. Knot the ends of the twine.

6. Let it dry. Decorate the top of the drumskin with acrylic paints or permanent markers.

The drumsticks can be sanded to round their edges, or you can wrap them with scraps of leather and tie them with decorative beads or feathers.

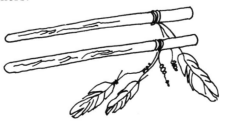

The Song of the Drum

In winter, the northern land was often buried under snow. Days were short, and darkness fell early. The earth lay cold and silent, as though sleeping until spring.

Gathered inside their shelters, drawn close around a snapping fire, the first people told stories and sang songs. A deep, strong drumbeat added rhythm to their voices.

Everywhere in North America, early people made drums. Their first drums were simple, probably not much more than a tree stump someone thumped with a stick. Later, perhaps someone discovered that a hollow log wrapped with a tight-fitting animal skin made a more pleasing sound.

As time passed, people improved and decorated their drums. Drums and drumsticks became beautiful objects. They were often painted, carved, or inlaid with shell or stone. Plain or ornate, since ancient times, the drum has been as basic to music as the human voice.

How Coyote Got His Medicine Power

Coyote the Unhappy Bachelor

Many legends say that it was Coyote who taught the tribes of the Northwest Coast how to catch and cook salmon. Sometime after that, old Coyote decided he should marry a young girl.

Coyote went from town to town, walking along the riverbanks, looking for someone to be his bride. The salmon swam beside him in the water. Wherever the people were kind to him, he made the river very narrow, so it would be easy for them to catch salmon from the banks.

But some chiefs did not think Coyote should marry a young girl. They would not agree to it because they thought he was too old. He even asked some girls, and they all said "no" too.

Coyote finally gave up on his idea of becoming a husband. But he wasn't happy about it, and he punished the people in the towns that had refused him. He created waterfalls in the rivers that brought salmon to their villages. The salmon could not jump over the falls and continue swimming upriver on their journeys to the villages.

So Coyote lived without a wife and the people of those towns went without salmon in their part of the river.

(This is a version of a popular Northwest Indian story.)

In the beginning of the world, Spirit Chief called a meeting of all animal people.

"Some of you do not have names yet," he said when they had gathered together. "And some of you do not like the names you have now. Tomorrow, before the sun rises I will give a new name to everyone. And I will give each an arrow also.

"Come to my lodge as soon as the darkness is gone. The one who gets there first may choose any name he wants, and I will give him the longest arrow. The longest arrow will mean that he will have the most power."

As the people left the meeting, Coyote said to his friend Fox, "I'm going to be there first. I don't like my name. I want to be called Grizzly Bear or Eagle."

Fox laughed. "No one wants your name. You may have to keep it."

"I'll be there first," repeated Coyote. "I won't go to sleep tonight."

That night he sat by his fire and stayed awake for a long time. Owls hooted at him. Frogs croaked in the marshes. Coyote heard them all. But after the stars had closed their eyes, he became very sleepy. His eyelids grew heavy.

"I will have to prop my eyes open."

So he took two small sticks and propped his eyelids apart. "Now I can stay awake."

But soon he was fast asleep, and when he awoke, the sun was making shadows. His eyes were dry from being propped open, but he ran to the lodge of Spirit Chief.

"I want to be Grizzly Bear," he said, thinking that he was the first one there. The lodge was empty except for Spirit Chief.

"That name is taken, and Grizzly Bear has the longest arrow. He will be chief of the animals on earth."

"Then I will be Eagle."

"That name is taken, and Eagle has the second arrow. Eagle will be chief of the birds."

"Then I will be Salmon."

"That name is taken, and Salmon has the third arrow. Salmon will be the chief of all fish. Only the shortest arrow is left, and only one name—Coyote."

And the Spirit Chief gave Coyote the shortest arrow. Coyote sank down beside the fire of the Spirit Chief. His eyes were still dry. The Spirit Chief felt sorry and put water in his eyes. The Coyote had an idea.

"I will ask Grizzly Bear to change with me."

"No," said Grizzly, "I cannot. Spirit Chief gave my name to me."

Coyote came back and sank down again beside the fire in the big lodge. Then Spirit Chief spoke to him.

"I have special power for you. I wanted you to be the last one to come. I have work for you to do, and you will need this special power. With it you can change yourself into any form. When you need help, call on your power.

"Fox will be your brother. He will help you when you need help. If you die, he will have the power to bring you back to life.

"Go to the lake and get four tules [bullrushes]. Your power is in the tules. Then do well the work I will give you to do."

So that is how Coyote got his special power.

People of California

24

A Home in the Earth

Overlooking the valley, the Maidu built their homes.

Once the land was not called California. It was called k'odo, earth. There were valleys, rivers, hills, and mountains. The land was inhabited by animals called "all our relations" and people—valley people, foothill people, and mountain people. Today these people are known as the Maidu.

It was spring in the valley. The air was warm. Black oak trees were again covered in leaves. Meadows were laced with yellow buttercups and sweet clover. There were grasshoppers and quail in the high grass. Red-crested woodpeckers and waterfowl sliced through the air. Deer grazed in open meadows. Salmon and trout darted through rivers that raced down canyons and fanned out across the broad valley floor.

Overlooking the valley, the Maidu built their homes, or earthlodges, on gentle slopes along creeks and rivers. The earthlodges were grouped in clusters, or communities, facing south to take the greatest advantage of the sun's warmth. A village was made up of several families. Between fifteen and five hundred people lived in each village.

The people called their earthlodge a *k'umum*. The frame of the *k'umum* was made of wood, was round in shape, and was covered with branches, reeds, and earth. It was built over a pit about three to four feet deep. The pit kept families warm in the winter by trapping heat from cooking fires.

In spring, indoor protection was only needed when it rained. Most of the time life was lived outdoors. Families lived under brush-covered porches built near the earthlodges.

Children played among the lodges and barrel-shaped acorn granaries. Men and women did their chores under an endless blue sky. The land was abundant with food waiting to be harvested.

It is morning. A group of women hike down into the valley to a field of rye grass. They are followed by girls and small children. The women's bone and wooden earrings, tipped with woodpecker and quail feathers, sway back and forth as they walk. Each woman wears a cap that is made of slender green rushes. Aprons of bark strips, or wire grass, hang about the women's waists. Some wear buckskin moccasins, while others go barefoot.

Each woman holds a seed beater and a basket-tray. On their backs are burden baskets woven from sturdy young willow. The basket is held in place by a strap connected to the basket and placed over the forehead.

The women disappear into the field of tall rye grass. Young girls watch as the women sweep their scoop-shaped seed beaters across the grass tops. The seed beater releases the grass seeds that fall and are caught in the trays.

The women give thanks because the rye seed is so plentiful. When the trays are full, the seeds are poured into their burden baskets. The baskets become heavy as the women move through the field.

That same morning, down by the river, the men watch as a shaman, or spiritual leader, jabs a two-pronged spear through the water and into a salmon. The shaman raises the salmon into the air. It is the first to be caught this year. The shaman honors the salmon, who are to give up their lives to be food. Now the fishing season can begin!

A seven-year-old boy watches his father place a bag-shaped net in the water. He holds apart the two ends of the willow rod to keep the net open. The father waits. He wears long, straight hair. A buckskin cloth is wrapped around his waist, and two feathers pierce his nose.

Fish swim inside the father's net. When they have traveled far enough inside he brings the ends of the willow rod together. The entrance is closed. The fish are trapped inside.

The father lifts the net out of the water. He gives thanks for his catch and checks to make sure none of the fish are females, because they are carrying eggs. To keep a fish that can help create more fish is disrespectful to the fish and endangers the survival of the people.

It is also disrespectful to waste salmon meat. To avoid this, women place the salmon on poles in the sun to be dried. Then they will grind the fish into powder. This powder is stored in baskets, to be eaten during the next winter or several winters to come.

Spring is a time of gathering for another winter. It is a time to be thankful for life in a land of abundance.

Village Clusters

The Maidu lived in village clusters. Each cluster consisted of a number of smaller villages built around one larger village. The size of this cluster depended on the size and number of families. But no matter how big or small, each one was always located near running water.

The people built anywhere from seven to fifty earthlodges. Next to each earthlodge was a barrel-shaped wooden structure. This structure, a granary, was used to store acorns and other foods, such as seeds. The granaries were often coated with pine pitch to prevent rodents from getting to the stored foods.

Women sweep their seed beaters across the grass.

The Bear Dance

Children chased after him with willow switches.

There Are No "Maidu"

In truth, there is no tribe called "Maidu." These central California Indians did not think of themselves as a tribe, but as the people, different from and perhaps superior to other groups. The word *Maidu* comes from the name they called themselves, *maydi*, which means person.

Though there are no ancient diaries recalling a Bear Dance, we are fortunate that Marie Potts, a Maidu woman and leader, born in 1895, in a mountain Maidu community in Big Meadow, California, has written about a Bear Dance she attended:

"The call for the dance was sent out by means of a knotted string; the knots numbered the days to go before the ceremony. Each day a knot was cut off. . . . The host group prepared huge quantities of food; the women ground acorns, cooked mush and acorn bread, gathered bulbs, seeds, and greens. The men scoured the valley and hills for game and for fish and wildfowl.

"The big day of the ceremony started with a sunrise raising of the Maidu flag and prayers, then greetings between the hosts and guests. Next to the pole for the flag another pole was planted from which a bearskin was suspended. The white goose feathers hanging from the chin indicated peace and purity. Assembled about these symbols, the people listened in silence to the prayers. . . . Next, breakfast was served, for some guests had arrived early and had camped along the way. After the visiting was over, games of all kinds were played until the people were called to dinner. After dinner the Bear Dance called *wahdom buyam* took place.

"One person was designated to wear a bearskin and to imitate a bear. He smelled and scratched the ground, pretending to look for food as he was a very hungry bear after hiber-

nating all winter. Children saw him in the arena [dance pit] and chased after him with willow switches, and he scampered around and frolicked with the children until he was tired. During this performance those who wished to take part formed a big circle around the bear and children. With a sign from the bear the singers started singing, and the dance began with the old people offering prayers. Visitors were invited to join in, and all able people took part in friendship. All dancers carried [fragrant] wormwood, which symbolized peace and friendship; the branches were held in their hands and swung in rhythm to the music.

"At the conclusion of the prayers and dancing the bear led the way, making a complete circle around the entire area. A leader picked up the flag and followed the bear, giving thanks and asking godspeed for those who would be journeying to their homes. As they paraded, the people hit sticks together, making as much noise as possible. The bear then led the way to a stream nearby where garlands [which had been worn] and greenery were thrown into the water, after which everyone washed their faces. This symbolized the throwing away of all bad feelings and of hopes for a new start with love and friendship for all; it marked the end of the ceremony. The flag and the bearskin were restored to their poles in the center of the dance lodge until evening. Then they were taken down and put away with a special prayer."

PLAYING THE HAND GAME

No celebration was complete without the game of chance called the Hand Game. This game, or forms of this game, was—and still is—played by Indian men and women throughout North America. The men and women, however, do not play the game together.

The object of the game was for one side to guess who, on the other side, held two marked bones or a ball in their hands.

The Maidu did not all play the Hand Game the same way. The Valley Maidu played the game in a circle, passing a ball between champion players.

Mountain Maidu had two groups of players sit lined up, facing each other behind a pole. Sometimes the players were made up of whoever wanted to gamble. Other times villages, or families, played against each other.

In the space between the poles the players put what they planned to wager. During the game the players used the poles as percussive instruments to accompany the songs they sang.

Each side started with ten sharpened sticks, or counters. There were also four bones made from solid or hollow sticks. Two of these bones had cord wrapped around the sticks' middles. Each side chose two champion players to represent each side.

One side began. The pair of champions quickly passed the bones back and forth between them, trying to baffle their opponents.

Songs were sung. Poles were struck against the ground, creating a steady, driving rhythm. Hands were in motion.

The air was swirling with songs and sounds. The side that held the bones signaled the other side to guess. Which hands of their champions held the marked bones? Guess.

If the guess was incorrect, the guessing side gave up one of their counters. This counter was stuck in the ground between the players, so everybody knew the score. If the guess was correct, the side holding the bones gave up a counter and the bones.

The game continued, sometimes all night. The first side to have all twenty counters won the articles on the ground.

My Hand Game

Here's a version of the Hand Game you can play.

You Will Need:
Twenty counters, represented by thin, fallen branches; a jacks or similar-sized ball; two 2-foot branches; a coin; and items to wager (a note promising to do the other person's chores on Saturday, fruit, snack foods). No money or valuable items can be wagered.

1. The players sit behind their 2-foot branches, facing each other. There should be no more than 2 feet of space between them. In this space the players place the articles brought to wager.

2. The players choose a song they both know and start singing.

3. The player who holds the ball moves it between his or her hands, trying to confuse the other player. The player who is guessing watches carefully, while striking his or her stick on the ground to the song's beat.

4. The player with the ball can, at any time, stop moving the ball and say, "guess." The other player must guess.

5. If the guess is correct, the player who is guessing receives one stick and the ball. The stick is pushed into the sand, or grass, between them. Or, if the game is being played indoors, the sticks can simply be placed between the two players. If the player who is guessing is incorrect, a stick is given to the player holding the ball.

6. The first person to have all twenty sticks wins the wagered articles.

They quickly passed the bones back and forth.

Hunters Honored the Deer

The chief of the village called for a deer hunt. This was a solemn decision. The animals and the people were connected. They lived on the same land and ate some of the same foods. The spirit that existed in animals was united with the spirit in the people. It was the same spirit.

If the people wanted to take the lives of the deer, this could not be done without giving something to the deer in return. The people honored the spirit connected to the deer with prayers, dances, and songs.

These rituals were performed exactly the same way before every hunt. This guaranteed the spirit connected to the deer would not be offended. It also guaranteed, because the Maidu had no books, that each generation would remember how to perform the ritual correctly.

If the people, at any time, didn't perform each ritual with the utmost seriousness, the connection between the deer and the people could be broken. Like two beads on a string, cut the string and the deer and the people could go their separate ways forever. The deer might no longer give up their lives to be food for people. The greatest hunter would be unable to kill a deer.

A hunter knew he was powerless unless he honored the spirit connected to the deer. Before every hunt, men gathered in the sweathouse. The smoke hole, which allowed smoke from the fire to leave through the roof, was blocked with buckskin.

A fire was started. The men sat on leaves and logs. The lodge became increasingly warmer. The men sang chants. These chants honored the spirit. The air became hot and filled with smoke. The hunters began to sweat.

Sweating purified the hunters' minds and their bodies. It removed all thoughts not connected to the deer and the hunt. This honored the spirit connected to the deer. Sweating also removed the smell that would scare the deer away during the hunt. When it got too hot, the men left the sweathouse and dived into a nearby lake or stream.

The hunters were ready. The people had done all they could to honor the spirit. There was nothing left to do but hunt.

The hunters picked up their weapons. Now they gathered their weapons. Some had bows in their hands and arrows stored in an animal-skin quiver, or pouch, hanging from their shoulders. Other hunters held clubs.

The hunters left the village. They walked to where deer were often seen. A deer herd was spotted. A portion of the hunters hid themselves among the trees and brush, along a path the deer used to go from one grazing area to another. They took out arrows from their quivers and placed them under their arm. They waited for the deer to come.

The other hunters drove the deer down the familiar path toward the hunters. The hunters fired their arrows and swung their clubs. Some of the younger deer would escape. Many of the older deer would be trapped.

This hunt was over. There would be others. And if the people continued to properly honor the spirit connected to the deer, the deer would let themselves be killed, until these hunters had enough food for the year ahead.

The Deer Did Not Die

The deer may have been killed, but the spirit connected to the deer did not die. It was everywhere. In every piece of clothing the people wore, in every piece of deer meat they ate, in every rattle they made, the spirit connected to the deer lived on together with the people's spirit.

The spirit connected to the deer was so important to the people that the animal was considered to be a member of the family. The people called the deer "my brother the deer." All animals were called by family names. They were "our relations."

Respected After Death

The Maidu respected the deer, even after its death, by using every part of the animal they could. The people made dried, roasted, and baked deer meat. Women tanned the deer's skin and created clothing, headbands, and belts. Men used the tendons, which connected the deer's muscles to its bones, as thongs to help connect parts of tools. The deer's bones were ground into meal. And the music in the deer's hooves was released by making them into rattles.

They fired their arrows and swung their clubs.

A Shaman's Work

The shaman removed the arrowhead from his mouth.

The Maidu, as all Indians, believed in the importance of keeping the earth in balance. If you took something from the earth, you gave something back.

When the earth did not provide an abundance of acorns one year, the Maidu knew they had not given enough back to the earth. Perhaps they had not properly honored the spirit connected to the acorn. This created an imbalance.

Gifted people, called shamans, had the power to restore the balance. They communicated with the spirits controlling the earth, and the health of the people. They healed the spirit that connected everything and everyone.

Believing in the Cure

In the north, both women and men shamans could cure the sick. Shamans saw illness as pain caused by diseased objects. An object, such as a stone, a small live animal, or an arrowhead, invaded the sick person's body. It created an imbalance in the person. The only way to restore balance was to remove this object.

The shaman placed himself into a trance. This trance was his transportation to the world of the spirits. There it was revealed which object was causing the disease.

With this knowledge, the shaman proceeded to heal the person. If the shaman found that an arrowhead was the disease-causing object, he might put an arrowhead in his mouth and lower his lips to where he believed the object entered the person's body.

The shaman then appeared to "suck" the arrowhead out of the person. The shaman removed the arrowhead from his mouth and showed it to the ill person. Sometimes it was covered in blood, giving the impression it had been removed from the person's body.

The ill person deeply believed there was an arrowhead inside his body that was causing the sickness. When the person saw the arrowhead come out of the shaman's mouth, it was as if it were the actual arrowhead. The person believed he was cured.

This was not trickery. Just as Western doctors believe that in order for patients to recover they must believe in the treatment, so it was with the shaman and an ill person.

Curing With Herbs

Shamans used a wide variety of herbs to cure illness. Well over two hundred drugs used today by Western doctors were also used by Indians. Today, Indians use a variety of methods to help them when they are ill, including Western medicine.

Below are some herbs used by Indian people of California to treat sickness:

Mountain Alder

Wild Buckwheat

Flowering Dogwood

Jimsonweed

American mistletoe

Oregon Grape

Alders: Dry rot from alder trees was mixed with powdered willow bark to treat burns.

Buckwheat: The dry seeds or leaves were eaten to relieve head- and stomachaches.

Dogwood: Tea from the roots was used as a cold remedy.

Jimsonweed: A cream was made from ground leaves. This cream was used on severe wounds and to relieve toothaches.

Mistletoe: The berries of the mistletoe were ground into a flour, mixed with water, and applied to the eyes to cure soreness and infection.

Oregon grape: A tea was made from the roots to increase a person's appetite.

Make a Clapper Rattle

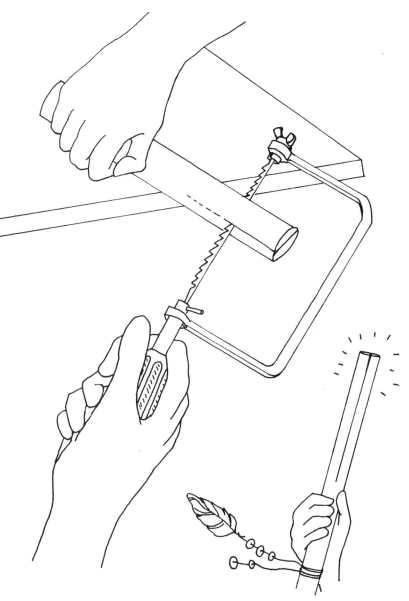

The rattle and the drum accompanied ceremonial dances and songs. A common rattle was the clapper rattle. It is easy to make.

You Will Need:

A bamboo pole, or a fallen branch, 1 inch thick; a saw; and an older person to help you.

1. Place the branch, or pole, on a raised flat surface, like a work bench or a picnic table. A small portion of the branch, or pole, should stick out over the edge of the bench or table.

2. Your older partner should begin sawing through the middle of this portion, while you hold the rest of the branch, or pole, against the flat surface. When your partner asks, slide another section of the branch, or pole, over the edge. Continue to do this until the branch, or pole, has been sawed almost in half lengthwise. At no time should you put your hands near the saw!

3. When this task has been completed, hold the "unsplit" portion of your clapper rattle in your hand and shake it from side to side. The rattle can also be slapped against your leg.

Listen to the rattle's sound. The Indians believed this sound was in the wood all the time, waiting to be released. You released it. The greater the care and respect you show for the wood while making this rattle, the purer the sound your rattle will make.

What was once an abandoned branch, or pole, sitting in silence, now makes music.

Coming of Age

Becoming a Young Woman

When a girl had her first menstrual period, it was an important event in her life. A close bond was formed between this girl and an older girl. The older girl would be the younger girl's friend, teacher, and source of comfort.

On the first day of the girl's period, she and her friend stood around a ring of pine needles with their heads covered. The ring was set on fire. The girls escaped the fire and ran a short distance away.

When they returned, there was a circle of women who sang, laughed, and gave the two young women a warm bath. Then, all the women went to the honored girl's house. For five nights, from dusk to dawn, the women celebrated with dancing and singing.

When the celebration was over, the joy of being accepted into the womanhood remained, along with five vertical red and black stripes painted on the young woman's cheek. These stripes would be removed over time. When the last stripe was erased, a girl was ready to get married.

The girls escaped the fire and ran a short distance away.

A Woman and Her Names

For the first several years of a child's life, Maidu parents called their son or daughter "baby," "girl," or "boy." When they knew their child better, parents created a name that matched the child's individual personality. Perhaps their child enjoyed climbing trees, or made noises in his or her sleep. Parents picked one of these qualities and gave the child a name such as "climbing girl" or "snoring bird."

This name, however, wasn't permanent. A girl would receive three names in her lifetime. She would be called by her first name until she had her first menstrual period. At this time she would receive a new name.

It was this name that would be with her during her courtship. If the young woman agreed to get married, in most cases, the man's parents sent gifts, such as clamshell beads, to the woman's parents. If the gifts were accepted, the man went to live with the woman's parents. He hunted and fished for them to prove he was a good provider. After six months, the couple went to live together with the man's parents. Living together meant they were married.

Out of this marriage came a family. When the woman became pregnant she would eat no meat or fish during her entire pregnancy. As she grew closer to giving birth she remained at home, and so did the husband.

When the child was born, a new chapter began in the woman's life. She was now a mother. And the name her husband had called her since their courtship was replaced with a new name.

Life continued. Years passed. And when the woman had grown old and her grandchildren were around her feet, she shed the name her children had called her for so many years and received her final name.

When death came, her body was placed in her finest clothing and buried along with her belongings and some food. Her "heart," or soul, left "like wind" from her mouth and then went back over every step in her life. Her soul "blew about," crying constantly. Finally, her soul left, guided by deceased relatives, into a paradise of food and pleasure where the creator, Kadyapam, lived.

A Man and His Name

A man's name changed only once in his life. He received his permanent name when he became a candidate for admission into the men's secret Kuksu cult.

Boys usually entered the cult at the age of fifteen. At that time they accepted their new names from a shaman, who received the names from the voice of a spirit. These new names were not revealed for eight days—until the boys were introduced into the cult at the ceremonial lodge.

The boys attended a meeting in the ceremonial lodge. When the meeting was over, the shaman did not let the candidates leave. He assigned each candidate a wand, and then he hung the wands inside the ceremonial lodge. He then sprinkled sacred acorn and birch-seed meal on the hair of each boy.

The shaman raced around the candidates, holding a stick from the fire and sprinkling water on them. He called out for food and goods. The older cult members entered the lodge and gave the candidates the gifts that the shaman asked for.

The following day, the boys began learning the cult dances. They were forbidden to eat any flesh. After eight days of instruction the candidates received their wands and their new names. They were *yephoni*, or members.

The new members were now allowed to wear a netted cap as an insignia of membership. They were also allowed to celebrate. Each new member gave a feast. The celebration lasted for days.

When it was over, the candidates were no longer boys. They were young men, ready to accept the responsibility of providing for and protecting their village. Soon they would be providers for their own families. Their lives would continue. And when they died, their "hearts" would be guided into a paradise of food and pleasure where the creator, Kadyapam, lived.

The Long and Short of It

Not all Maidu men wore their hair long. In some areas men had short hair. They didn't have scissors to cut their hair. Instead, men used hot embers to burn away unwanted hair. To comb their hair, people used beaten pine cones and porcupine tails as hairbrushes.

The shaman sprinkled sacred acorn and seed meal on the hair of each boy.

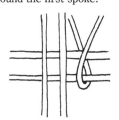

HOLDING LIFE

Baskets were used in almost every part of Maidu life. Women made baskets in several ways, and in many sizes, depending on the basket's purpose.

Basketmaking began with women searching the land for materials. Women gathered the inner bark of willow and cedar trees, along with young shoots from bushes, fern stems, tree roots, and grasses.

Whatever they took from the earth, they put something back in its place, like a pinch of tobacco. This made the earth complete again. It restored the balance. Other materials for baskets were traded for redbud shoots.

Women used their materials carefully. They made light, flexible baskets out of inner bark cattails. They made harder baskets from tougher materials, such as twigs.

Two methods were used to make a basket: twining or coiling. They used twining to make seed beaters, fish traps, and burden and storage baskets.

It was more difficult for women to coil baskets than twine them, but the effort was worth it. Coiling created firm, watertight baskets.

Cooking baskets had to be watertight. The people had no kettles or pots to boil water in. Water was boiled in cooking baskets by dropping fire-heated rocks into a cooking basket filled with water. Food was cooked by placing it in the boiling water.

Baskets: A Woven Canvas

Baskets were also a woven canvas upon which women made artwork. Designs were woven into many Maidu baskets. These designs were precisely crafted. Women measured their art, using knotted string, like lines in a ruler, to carefully evaluate each part of their design.

Designs were incorporated into the basket by replacing a natural willow root with one that had been darkened by burying it in mud, or with one that had been stained by acorns.

Make a Basket

No two baskets were exactly the same, because no two weavers were the same. Each basket, each bowl, mirrored the weaver's creativity and skill. Now it is your turn to be a weaver. Here is how to twine your own personal bowl.

You Will Need:

Basket weaving supplies, available from your local crafts store. Or, in your surrounding area you can look for long twigs. The twigs must be stripped of their bark and soaked overnight to make them more flexible. Most of the materials offered at the crafts store will also need to be soaked. Optional: feathers, shells, and beads.

1. Take four spokes, such as the twigs, and arrange them in a cross, as in the illustration.

2. Take one strand, or weaver, and bend it in half around the first spoke.

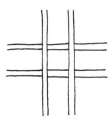

3. Give the weaver a half twist and then wrap it around the second spoke. Continue doing this around the other spokes, as shown in the illustration.

If you have not used up your weaver, continue twining. If you have used up your first weaver, pick up two new strands. These

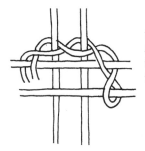

two strands will be your next weaver.

Hold one strand in each hand. Go to the spoke where the first weaver ended and push the ends of the two strands into the twining.

When they are secure, take the other side of the two strands and give them a half-twist around each spoke as you did before.

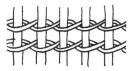

Continue adding weavers when necessary. You will notice that you are creating a spiral shape around the spokes.

Eventually you will need to add more spokes. Just add a spoke to each of the four corners and continue twining.

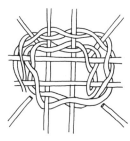

When you think your bowl is big enough, bend the loose ends of the spokes inside the bowl.

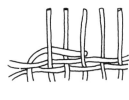

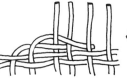

Take a string and wrap one end around one of the bent spokes several times. Then take the rest of the string and wrap it around the other bent spokes, one at a time. When you wrap the string around the last spoke, leave enough string to tie a knot. The bowl now has a rim. And you have a bowl. You can decorate your bowl with feathers, shells, and beads.

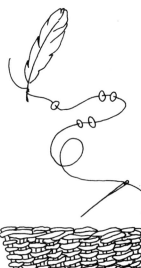

People of the Southwest

Spider Woman and Earth Mother

Hopi teachings say that the universe began with Taiowa (ti-OH-wah), the Creator. He was the Father, the Sun. The world was called Tokpela (tok-PAY-lah), Endless Space. It was a beautiful place, filled with spirits that lived happily with each other. Tokpela had no time, no shape, no beginning, and no end.

When it was time for the spirits to take human form and live on earth, Taiowa made a helper. He told his helper, Sotuknang (so-TU-knang), to make the new universes in proper order. Sotuknang took matter and made the form of earth. Then he made water and wind. Taiowa was pleased. Next he told Sotuknang to make life on earth. To help him, Sotuknang made Spider Woman.

Spider Woman mixed earth with saliva and made two beings. She covered them with wisdom. They were twins. Palongawhoya (pa-long-AH-hoy-ah) would keep the world in order, and Poqunghoya (po-KWUNG-hoy-ah) would create sound. The twins went to the North Pole and the South Pole, to keep the world rotating.

Spider Woman created trees, bushes, plants, flowers, seeds, nuts, birds, and animals. Over each one she sang the Creation Song. Tiowa, Sotuknang, and Spider Woman looked at everything. They liked it all. "It is ready for humans," Taiowa, the Creator, said.

Now Spider Woman gathered four colors: yellow, red, white, and black. She mixed them with saliva and sang the Creation Song over them. They became men. Then she created four more people, like herself. These women would be the men's partners. But they could not yet speak.

Spider Woman called the echo twin, who gave the First People their voices. He also gave them wisdom and the power to reproduce. He told them, "I have given you this world to live on and be happy. But you must do something for me. You must respect the Creator at all times. You must use your wisdom. Live in harmony, and love the Creator who made you. Never forget these things."

The people saw that the earth was like them, a living thing. The earth was their mother. She gave them corn, on which their lives depended. So they understood that their mother had two aspects: Earth Mother and Corn Mother. They knew that their father was the Sun. The people knew that they also had human parents, but Earth Mother—Corn Mother—and Father Sun were their *real* parents.

The people were happy. They filled the First World with their children. They understood the animals. But as time went on, they forgot the plan of Creation, their promises to use wisdom and to respect Taiowa, the Creator.

Sotuknang took the good people to a safe place. Then he destroyed the First World. Two more times he made beautiful new worlds for the people. But when they forgot how to live right, he destroyed the Second and Third Worlds too. Spider Woman always watched over the good people. But each new world was harder for them. While they were lost on the vast waters of the Third World, Sotuknang made the Fourth World.

The people crossed the water in every direction looking for land. All at once, the waters grew still. Gentle waves pulled their boats toward shore. The people knew that they had found the Fourth World. Filled with happiness, they rushed ashore. When everyone was out of the boats and gathered together, Sotuknang appeared.

"You are all here," he said. "This is good. You have found the place I made for you. You have come from the West. Those high flat mountains behind you are your footprints. Watch, while I destroy them."

Sotuknang had one more thing to tell the people. He told them that the new world was not beautiful like the others. It had good and bad, hot and cold, beauty and barrenness. He told them to go in four directions and claim the earth for the Creator.

Before they started, the people divided into four clans. Each would migrate in a different direction. This was Tuwaqachi (tuh-wah-KAH-chee), Fourth World, World Complete.

Filled with happiness, they rushed ashore.

KOKOPELI, THE FLUTE PLAYER

He raised his flute and began to play a sweet melody.

Hopi legends say that the people migrated to every corner of the earth before they found the Fourth World, which became their final home. Led by two *mahus* (ma-HOOZ), locustlike insect people (some say they were ants), a group of Hopi climbed to the top of a mountain. At the top they met an eagle. He clutched two arrows in his claws. He looked at the two *mahus*. Each one was carrying a flute. Eagle told them they could only live there if they passed two tests that he would give them.

Eagle said to the first *mahu*, "I am going to poke you in the eye with these arrows. If you do not close your eyes, you and the people who follow you may live here." The *mahu* did not even blink as the arrows touched his eye. This surprised Eagle.

"You are a very brave people," he said. "But the next test is much harder, and I do not think you can pass it." He drew back the bow and aimed his third arrow, shooting it deep into the *mahu*'s body. The wounded *mahu* appeared unharmed. He raised his flute and began to play a sweet melody. Eagle was amazed at this power.

He took his fourth arrow and shot the second *mahu*. He, too, began playing tender music on his flute.

Both *mahus*, with arrows piercing their sides, continued playing their lovely, gentle music. The flutes' soothing notes lifted their spirits and healed their wounded bodies.

Eagle was pleased. He told the people they could settle on this land. He said that when they wanted to talk to Father Sun, the Creator, they could use his eagle feather, and he would deliver their message.

The locust *mahus* were given the name *Kokopeli*, the Humpbacked Flute Player. In the Hopi language, *koko* means stick or wood, and *pilau* means hump, good descriptions for the wooden-looking hump of the locust and the stick flute he carried.

Whenever the people were sad, Kokopeli would come to play his flute, sing, and dance. After many years, he became a kachina spirit. And as the Hopi settled and began planting corn, Kokopeli, like all kachinas, was there to dance in the fields and bring rain.

Make a Flute

See if your library owns—or will borrow—a recording of traditional Indian flute music. A Navajo named R. Carlos Nakai is one among many Native American musicians who has recorded traditional music.

An authentic wood or clay Indian flute costs hundreds of dollars. But you can make your own. With a little practice, you can create nice melodies.

This project requires some woodworking tools and a grownup who can help you with drilling.

What You Need:
Materials and equipment: a 12-inch tube made of plastic (PVC pipe or an old snorkel), bamboo, or wood; a grownup to help you; a saw (if the tube needs to be shortened); a knife; a drill with a ¼-inch bit, for blowhole and finger holes; a round file; a cork to fit into the end of the tube (corks are usually available at craft or kitchen equipment stores, or where winemaking or chemical supplies are sold).

1. Cut the tube to 12 inches.
2. Place the cork in the hole at one end. (If you are using bamboo, leave a joint at one end and sand the rest of the inside, using sandpaper taped around a small dowel.)
3. Measure and mark 1½ inches from the corked end, and drill a ¼-inch hole. This will be the mouthpiece hole (blowhole). Enlarge it with the file until the blowhole is an oval, ½ inch across. See diagram A.
4. Toward the end opposite the blowhole, drill six finger holes. For a flute that makes primitive, individual style sounds, space the holes where your index, middle, and fourth fingers fit comfortably. For a traditional scale, space holes according to diagram B.
5. File or sand any rough edges.

How to Play:
Hold the flute so the blowhole is close to your mouth and the flute extends sideways. If you are right-handed, place the index, middle, and fourth fingers of your *left* hand over the first three holes (closest to the blowhole) and the index, middle, and fourth fingers of your right hand over the last three finger holes.

Practice blowing over the blowhole with a steady breath until you get sound. Experiment with tone by closing different finger holes as you play. For detailed playing instructions, you can find a book that teaches the musical scale and a finger chart for the flute.

A.

blowhole

finger holes

cork

B.

blowhole

traditional fingerholes

C 1" A 1" G 1" F 7/8" E 7/8" D 2"

cork

B thumbhole

Gray Stones on the High Mesa

He chose carefully, setting each stone in place.

Huge white clouds drifted across the sky. They cast soft shadows across the land, hiding the hot sun. Poli (POH-lee) worked alone beside a pile of gray stone slabs he had cut from a nearby hillside. Stone by stone, the young Hopi man chose carefully, setting each one in place, along the walls of the dwelling he was building. Between the large stones he set smaller ones, sometimes breaking them into chunks with his stone axe.

When several stones were lined in a neat row, Poli scooped his hands full of sand and clay he had mixed with water in a shallow pit in the ground. He packed the mortar into the spaces between the slabs. More stones followed, and more mortar. He left a small rectangular opening in each wall for daylight to enter. His house was taking shape.

Around him, he heard other men chipping stones to build their houses. Sometimes they paused to help one another. Poli stopped to drink from a clay jug. As he rested, his eyes scanned the land around him. It was a rocky, windswept place, with few trees. Instead, the ground was dotted with spiky yucca plants, prickly-pear cactus, and sagebrush.

The Hopi had found this spot after a long journey. They had looked in all directions. From here the land fanned out to the south in three directions, each forming a long, flat plateau, called a *mesa* (MAY-suh), that rose high above the valley. On it they were building the new Hopi village, the *pueblo*, where their families would live for hundreds of years to come.

Where Are the Hopi Mesas?

Mesa (MAY-suh) was originally a Spanish word that means plateau or tabletop. It describes an elevated land form with a flat surface and steep sides. It is different from a mountain, whose top forms a peak. The top of a mesa is flat and wide. Three mesas in northeastern Arizona have been the homeland of the Hopi people since prehistoric times. In the north, Black Mesa rises two thousand feet above the surrounding land. Toward the south, the elevation drops gradually and the land is gouged into three long fingers. The Hopi settled on these three southern mesas, which are now part of the Hopi Reservation. White explorers gave them the names First, Second, and Third mesas.

There are eleven pueblo villages on these mesas, and a twelfth in a nearby valley, where the Hopi still live in homes built of stone and follow many of the traditions handed down from their ancestors.

For hundreds of years, narrow dirt paths connected the mesas to each other. Today they can also be reached by roads.

Before the walls of Poli's house were finished, he made many trips into the mountains beyond the mesa to cut cedar poles for a ladder and for the roof beams of his house. The long cedar beams, laid across the walls, supported the heavy earthen roof. The ladder leaned against the outside wall, leading to the only entrance, which was in the roof.

To smooth the outer surface and seal it against the weather, Poli plastered his house with a thick layer of mud and clay. At last it was finished. It had taken many days, and now it stood solid beneath the endless sky.

When the wind whipped across the mesa, the Hopi were sheltered by the thick walls of their homes. When snow buried the earth under a blanket of white, they had fires to keep warm. When it rained, they gave thanks. They believed that they should live in balance and harmony with all things. Even the name "Hopi" reminded them of this. It means "the peaceful ones."

In the valley below the mesa, the Hopi planted small gardens. They could not see the water that flowed beneath the earth's surface, but they knew it was there. They poked seed holes nearly one foot deep and planted corn, beans, melon, and squash. The seeds found moisture and grew strong. To help their crops, the Hopi danced and said prayers. They trusted Earth Mother to provide them with food and water, and she did.

The Sun Turns Back

High in the mountains above the Hopi village on First Mesa, three mysterious figures appear. Elder Brother, the tallest one, leads the way down a path spread with cornmeal, toward the village. In one hand he carries a staff—a walking stick—with turkey feathers and an ear of corn fastened to it. In his other hand is a flat stick, carved with the corn design.

Elder Brother is bare chested. A green mask covers his face. One side is decorated with a green and black horn. On the other is a fan. His arms and legs are painted with white stripes. He wears a knee-length kilt.

The two figures walking with him wear masks and kilts too. They are both wrapped in white wool blankets. They are Blue Corn Girl and Yellow Corn Girl, Elder Brother's sisters. But the "sisters" are not women. All three are Hopi men, taking the form of sacred spirits. These three ancient spirits, and many others who will appear in the coming months, are called kachinas (kah-CHEE-nahz).

These three who have come from the mountains today are the first kachinas of the year. They are an important part of Hopi life. In fact, to the Hopi, kachinas *are* life. But on this cold winter evening, no one comes out to greet them. Grains of dry snow whirl over the frozen ground. Darkness comes early. The streets of the *pueblo* are deserted.

It is the Winter Solstice. Two days ago, the Sun Watcher told the Hopi chief that the shortest day was coming. Then the chief announced the first kachina ceremony. It is called Ta'wa A'hoyi, the Sun Turns Back. It means that soon the days will begin to grow lighter, longer, and warmer. The Winter Solstice brings the kachinas back again, to teach and guard the people.

Preparing for a New Growing Season

Many men have gathered in the kiva (KEE-vah), the chief's prayer house. For four days, the men will go without eating. They will pray, sing, and make offerings, asking the sun to remember them and bless them as he makes his way back across the earth.

For several days, the men will ask for blessings on their homes, for enough rainfall, and for other things they need. They will make offerings with objects that hold symbolic meaning, such as pine needles, willow twigs, and sage. Every offering has bird feathers and a bit of cornhusk attached to it. Inside each husk is ground cornmeal and honey.

Women rarely enter the kivas. For the first kachina ceremony, which they will not see, they fill a large basket with corn that will be taken into the kiva. Each woman makes a bundle of three ears, to be placed on a cloth near the altar.

Inside the kiva, Elder Brother, Blue Corn Sister, and Yellow Corn Sister perform their parts in a long drama that includes the sun's return and the departure of ice and snow. Men in other sacred costumes join the ceremony.

Sharing the Gifts

The ritual of the fourth night lasts until dawn, when the men take the offerings they made and go into the village, leaving some in homes, some at the farms, some with the animals. The women come and get the corn that was taken into the kiva.

In each home, the corn bundles are placed on top of all the other seed corn in the home. The three special ears will be the first seeds planted in the spring, to prepare the way for a healthy and abundant corn crop.

The men have one last duty. Using willow branches and four feathers, they make Sun prayer sticks. On the last day of the Sun Turns Back ceremony, the prayer sticks are gathered into a white blanket. A messenger takes them four miles east of the First Mesa village, to an altar called the Sun House. He places them on the altar, facing the east, so the morning sun will shine on them. The first kachina ceremony is over.

These Hopi kachina dolls are, from left to right, Crow Mother, Hilili, and Picharuhu.

Make a Spirit Figure

If you were going to make a spirit figure that had special meaning for you, what would it be?

Real kachina dolls were made from the roots of the cottonwood tree. They were carved with feet and detailed masks and costumes. But your spirit figure can be made from anything at all. It can have a mask or not. You can decorate it with stones, feathers, fake fur, paper cutouts, or anything that expresses your feelings.

When you finish it, keep it someplace where you can see it. It shows what you care about.

What You Need:

For the body, start with an empty paper towel tube, a one-quart milk carton, a wooden dowel, or a tied bundle of dried grasses. Make hair and facial features using cotton puffs, twine, buttons, shells, or fancy pasta shapes. Make slits in the body and poke plastic straws or feathers into the slits, or wrap the body with layers of colored yarn. Tie small objects to the yarn, or hold them in place as you wrap several layers of yarn over them. Secure the yarn with white glue (it dries clear and hard).

Or make an ocean or forest kachina by wrapping the tube in twine or yarn and decorating it only with natural objects you would find at the beach or in the woods. Smear sections of the tube with white glue and roll it in sand, pine needles, or crushed leaves, and then add things you find when you go exploring.

The Snake Dance

Great crowds came to Oraibi.

This account, by Don C. Talayesva, a Hopi Sun Chief, describes how hard it was to be brave during the Snake Dance.

"My earliest memories of my . . . grandfather, Homikniwa, are full of kind feelings. . . . In the mornings before sunrise he sang to me and told me stories. He took me to his fields, where I helped him to work or slept under a peach tree. Whenever he saw me make a circle on the ground he stepped cautiously around it, saying that he had to watch me lest I block his path with my antelope power. He kept reminding me of this power. He also took me through the fields to collect healing herbs. I watched him sprinkle cornmeal and pray to the Sun god before picking off leaves or berries or finding medicine roots.

"In late summer when I was perhaps four, the men in the Snake and Antelope societies placed signs outside their kivas and our parents warned us to stay away. For several days the men came out in fancy costumes . . . and marched off the mesa in search of snakes. I wished to follow them and was told that some day I might be chosen as a Snake man. In the evenings the people told how many snakes had been caught and that some were large rattlers. We knew snakes were spirit gods who bring rains and never harm anyone with a good heart. [At the Snake Dance], we were told never to act silly and scream . . . when a snake [comes] toward us. My grandfather said such foolish behavior spoiled the ceremony. When snakes were pleased with their treatment they were quiet and would bring rain as a reward.

"On the last day of the ceremony great crowds . . . came to Oraibi [a village on Third Mesa]. They climbed over housetops, stood in doorways, and crowded into the plaza near the Snake kiva to see everything. Late in the afternoon the Antelope men entered the plaza in fine costumes and marched around the Snake house [*kisi*] four times, stamping their feet before it. Then the Snake members, painted and finely dressed, came with lively steps and circled the *kisi* in the same manner. Soon they were dancing with big live snakes in their hands and between their teeth. Some snakes wriggled and stuck out their tongues, but others were quiet. My grandfather said later that dancers with the best hearts had the quietest snakes. When the serpents were placed in a circle on the ground, they ran in every direction before the snake catcher could get them. . . . A bull snake came toward me at the edge of the plaza. I did not cry, but I was ready to run when the snake catcher picked it up. He was brave and had a good heart. I wanted to be a Snake man. . . ."

About Those Snakes

The thought of *seeing* a few dozen rattlesnakes and bull snakes, much less *catching* them, doesn't appeal to everybody. But the Pueblo people welcomed the snake ceremony. Snakes, the Hopi believe, bring the rain.

Before the ceremony, the men in the village hunt snakes for four days, each day in a different direction, poking the bushes and checking behind rocks. When they catch one, it is sprinkled with sacred cornmeal and placed in a bag.

Rattlesnakes are not defanged for the ceremony. But for several weeks before the event, the men who will handle them take a special herb found in the desert. They say it keeps them healthy if they are struck by a rattler.

As the ceremony begins, the snakes are brought to a priest in the center of the plaza. As a male dancer passes the priest, he is given a snake, which he puts between his teeth. Another dancer comes with him, carrying a stick with many eagle feathers. Waving the feathers, which represent large birds—the snake's mortal enemies—or brushing the snake on the head with the stick keeps it from biting.

When the dancing is over, the snakes are heaped in the center of the plaza, on a rain symbol made of cornmeal. Feathered sticks keep the snakes in the circle. Finally, the snakes are carried to the edge of the mesa and let go. They race to the east, west, north and south. Hurrying in the four directions of the universe, the snakes will go underground, asking the Water God to bring rain.

They danced with big live snakes between their teeth.

A HOPI CALENDAR

These kachinas are waiting to dance in Powamu, *or the "Bean-planting" Ceremony.*

December started the Hopi calendar with an event marked by tribal people everywhere, the Winter Solstice. The Hopi Winter Solstice ceremony ended with a four-day feast of rabbit stew, squash, melon, and cornmeal cakes.

The first moon of **January** brought nighttime kachina dances inside the kivas, warmer than in the frosty air outside. To celebrate returning birds, Hummingbird, Mockingbird, Canyon Wren, Bee and Butterfly kachinas, and many others in spectacular feathers danced in the firelight.

In **February**, a nine-day bean ceremony celebrated the sprouting of new bean and corn crops. Seeds that were ceremonially "forced" (planted early, inside, so

they would sprout faster) were carried through the village on trays. The children had not seen the planting. They were astounded to see seedlings growing in winter. They were told that the kachinas grew the beans in the mountains.

The Bean Dance was the first outdoor dance of the year. It was also the first time children saw kachinas without their masks, and figured out that men were acting the part of kachinas.

The dance was also special because young people could give gifts to each other. If a girl at the dance gave a sweet cornmeal cake to a boy, she wasn't just being nice. She was telling him she would like to become his wife.

In **March**, clowns ran

through the village, telling everyone that the kachinas were coming again and the men must do the cooking for a change.

During **April**, **May**, and **June**, there were plaza dances while the crops were being planted. For sixteen nights, men practiced their dances and songs, and prepared their masks and costumes in the kivas. On the day of each dance, visitors came from nearby villages to watch the kachinas perform.

Finally, in late **June** or **July**, near the Summer Solstice, the Homegoing Ceremony took place. Now the kachinas would leave the people and return to their own homes, to plant their own crops. They came into the village, as always, on a path strewn with sacred cornmeal. Though the kachinas brought gifts for everyone,

the last dance was a solemn time.

As the dance ended, the young women who had married during the year came into the plaza, dressed in their wedding clothes. This was the only kachina dance they attended that year. When it ended, they put their wedding dresses away for the rest of their lives.

Although the kachinas left in midsummer, the ceremonies did not end. It took several weeks to prepare for the important Snake-Antelope Dance in **August**, and the Flute Ceremony, with prayers for rain and prosperity.

The last two dances were the Women's Dance in **September**, with rituals of fertility, and the Women's Basket Dance in **October**, marking the end of the Hopi ceremonial year.

First Pottery

Talatawi (ta-la-TAH-wee), whose Hopi name means Song to the Morning Sun, stood very still while her mother finished twisting her long black hair into a "butterfly whorl" of two wide twists at the sides.

When her hair was done, Talatawi wrapped a shawl around her shoulders. Her father had finished weaving the shawl for her yesterday. He wove all the fabric for his family's clothes, including the brown cotton dress his daughter had put on this morning. It was top-stitched with bright red thread, but sewn together only at the right shoulder, leaving Talatawi's left arm free for working. A black sash wound around Talatawi's waist and hung in a fringe at one side.

From the corner of the cool adobe, the young girl found a heavy cloth. Tucking it under one arm, she went outside. The morning sunlight streaked brightly across the flat-topped hills. When she reached her cousin's house, Cho'ro was waiting.

The two dark-haired girls followed the path that led away from the village, down into a sandy canyon below First Mesa. Jackrabbits and quail darted through the low brush, scurrying from the sound of the girls' chatter. They were talking about yesterday. At the plaza dance, Talatawi had smiled at Kwa'taka, Eagle Man. He, too, was young, but he had smiled back. Cho'ro thought Talatawi was fortunate. She was certain there would soon be a wedding in the family.

This morning the girls had many things to talk about. They were growing up, and beginning to do women's work by themselves. For the first time, they were gathering clay alone, and would make pottery without the help of their mothers. They knew where to get the best gray clay, almost a mile from their village.

As they entered the canyon, Talatawi and Cho'ro met other girls and women from First Mesa, carrying big pots of water from the spring to take back up to the village.

Stooping low, they crawled into a hollow in the canyon wall.

You Be the Potter

Hopi potters use several varieties of clay, depending on what the earth is like where they live. Using a stiff yucca brush, they often paint black, red-orange, and white geometric designs onto light-colored pots. Pots for everyday work are not decorated.

Working with potter's clay is fun, especially if you don't mind getting a little messy. Most art stores carry both red and gray earth clay. There's also a new kind of clay in craft stores that you might try. There are several brands, one of which is called Sculpy. It comes in small packages of many colors, and looks and feels like modeling clay. You don't add water to it as you do with natural clay, so there's no mess. You can fire it in the kitchen oven, at a very low temperature. Once you "cook" it, the shape is permanent.

You can sculpt objects of any shape you like, but to make tall vases or bowls, the coil method is recommended. The Hopi always used this classic technique. Roll the clay into coils, long "ropes," then coil them one by one in rings, sealing the ends where they meet. As you build the height, smooth the inside and outside surfaces. Bake it on a cookie sheet according to the package directions.

There was no water on First Mesa. Bringing it from the valley, like weaving baskets and making pottery, was a task the women did. Men did all the clothes weaving, tended the gardens, and led ceremonial dances. Everyone had different things to do.

When the cousins crossed the shallow trickle of water running between the rocks in the canyon, they were near the source of the clay. Stooping low, they crawled into a dark hollow in the canyon's wall. The clay ran in layers between streaks of sandstone. Spreading their cloths on the ground, they dug the cold clay from the earth. It was slow, hard work, but they helped each other. They piled the damp clay on one cloth and then the other, until both were full. They dug only enough clay to make a few pots.

The next morning while it was still cool, Talatawi and Cho'ro climbed up onto the roof of Talatawi's house. Families spent lots of time on the flat rooftops, drying food in the sun, weaving baskets, or listening to singers in the evening.

Talatawi began by rolling out long coils of clay. Around and around she wrapped them, sealing each coil where it met the next one. Working with a dry, curved gourd shell, she carefully scooped the inside of the pot, smoothing and rounding it until the shape pleased her. When her pot was tall and smooth, she dipped a rabbit tail into the *slip*—a liquid of finely ground clay and water—and applied several coats.

When the pot was dry, Talatawi began the last step. She would rub for hours, polishing the outside with small smooth pebbles until it was shiny. They did not throw out the leftover clay bits. The clay was carefully saved for next time, stored in a sack that was always kept damp.

When the new pots were dry, the girls built a fire of dried animal dung and wood chips that would smoulder for hours. They buried their new pots in the middle of the coals, setting them carefully on a bed of old broken pottery pieces.

The pots would bake for several hours. The girls felt tense, hoping none would crack.

Talatawi decided not to paint designs on her first pot. She would paint her others, but the first one seemed special. She would save it until she and Eagle Man were married. It would be the one she used every day, and only for mixing cornmeal.

They buried their new pots in the middle of the coals.

People of the Great Basin

Under the Sun

The family walked barefoot over the hardened ground.

    The Northern Paiute family broke camp. There was no more food. They had to find a new camp. They had to find more food. The family walked barefoot over the hardened earth, carrying their belongings.

    The land was dry and cracked. Patches of dried, tall grass cast shadows over stubby sagebrush and juniper. The hot wind swept loose dirt over the flat ground. The only water for miles was in a watertight bottle carried by the mother.

    The grandmother carried her cooking tools and baskets. The baskets were all empty except one, which was half-filled with delicate cattail seeds. It was the family's emergency food supply.

    The two sons, the mother, and the daughter carried the family homes in pieces. The two sons carried the poles, the frames of the houses. The mother and daughter carried the brittle reed-mat, which covered the frame.

    The father and grandfather carried only their bows and arrows. They had to be ready to chase any small animal that might cross their path. They watched for lizards and rats. They searched the ground for rabbit tracks. The entire family was watching. They were always watching.

    The daughter spotted the red berries of the desert thornbush. She rushed ahead of the rest of her family. The bushes held few berries. Other animals had gotten there first.

    The family put their belongings down. They gave thanks for what little food they found and they ate the remaining fruit. Each family member took a small sip of warm, stale water from the bottle. The mother spotted some grasshoppers. She and her daughter quickly got one of the baskets and moved to capture the insects before they got away.

The grandmother picked at the crusted ground with a stick, sharpened at one end, to reach one of the thornbush's roots. It was hard work. She cut a portion of the first root she came to and stored it in a basket.

The grandmother placed a stone in the space where the root had been. She had taken something from the earth. She had to give something back. The stone was not a poor replacement for the root. The stone, like the root, was alive. Both were connected to the same spirit.

While the women worked, the father and grandfather watched two lizards hiding behind a rock. The lizards were eyeing a berry the grandfather had placed in the open. The lizards raced for the berry. The father and grandfather pounced on the lizards. They caught one. The other got away.

It was time to move on. Each family member gathered what they had been carrying. They walked on comforted by the additional food they had found.

Several hours later they stood before a patch of rice grass. During the spring the grass was watered by a flowing stream. Now there was just enough water to fill a small pothole.

The grandfather, father, and his two sons set the poles in the ground, and tied them together. The mats were tied to the frames. The sun was setting. The women prepared what food they had. As the family worked, they listened and watched for a scampering jackrabbit or rat.

The family ate. They talked and joked. The grandmother praised her granddaughter for spotting the thornbush. The sun set. The pitch-black sky shone with a million stars. The family slept. They had found a new camp, for the moment.

Wearing What's Available

During the warm months, Paiute men wore a cloth around their waists. Women wore a thin apron of woven bark tassels around their waists as clothing. Sometimes families wore stiff sandals woven from sagebrush.

When bark could not be found, the women lifted the sheets of algae that formed on pools of idle water. When the sheets had dried, they cut them into the proper size strips to form an apron.

It was not unusual, however, for people to go without any clothing.

LIFE AMONG THE PIÑON TREES

When rose hips were ripening in the lowlands, the nuts of the piñon tree were ripening in the hills. And the people wondered what this year would bring. Would it be a harvest of plenty?

Each fall, families sent scouts into the hills to answer this question. These men traveled up to fifty miles searching for the piñon grove that contained the most cones. If the scouts found such a grove they returned, bringing a branch heavy with cones as proof of their discovery.

The families gathered up their belongings. This time they knew when they set up camp again it wouldn't be for a day, or a week, but for months. The scouts were correct. The families arrived to find the grove held an abundance of piñon nuts. The work began. Camp was set up.

This season's harvest was large. There was work for everyone. As the sun rose, families swept through the groves gathering cones. They knocked the cones to the ground, using long willow poles. Boys climbed the trees to harvest the cones by hand.

Cones fell like raindrops and covered the ground. Young women collected them in their burden baskets. They carried them to camp, to the fires tended by the older women.

The older women took over. They picked the nuts from the cones and placed them on flat baskets. They added hot coals, from the fire, to the baskets and immediately began shaking the baskets to roast the nuts. The red coals and the yellow nuts swirled together. The women never let the hot coals stay in one place. The baskets did not burn and the nuts were evenly roasted.

The heat caused the nuts to crack, revealing the kernels inside. The women pounded the kernels into a paste. From this paste, they would make a rich, oily soup.

For the next several months the harvest continued. As women mixed the coals and the nuts, families mixed work and pleasure. Knowing there was plenty to eat, they took naps or gambled during the hot afternoons. Young men and women talked of marriage. Old friends exchanged news and stories.

The past months of hardship were gone, for the time being.

First Give Thanks

When families reached the piñon grove in the hills, the first morning was spent giving thanks. The nuts of the first day's harvest were donated to the Piñon Prayer Dance. This dance began when the sun set and continued through the night. A shaman woman helped guarantee the success of the harvest by sending away all ghosts in the forest.

After this was accomplished, piñon nuts were spread on the ground in thanks to the earth. The dancers circled the campfire with a shuffling step. They prayed for rain so that the nuts wouldn't dry out. They also sang songs of thanks.

They knocked the cones to the ground, using willow poles.

Families drove the rabbits toward the nets.

A PLACE OF GATHERING

In November, the Northern Paiute families left the hills. They had gathered all the food they could. Now it was time to return to the flatlands. The rabbits had eaten well all summer. They were fat and ready to be hunted.

The men set long nets across wide stretches of land. Families drove the rabbits toward the nets, where they were killed with clubs and bows and arrows.

Rabbit meat was an important part of the Northern Paiute diet. Even more essential was the rabbit's fur. Without it there would be no material to make winter clothing.

Northern Paiute and the Shoshoni couldn't depend on the skins of larger animals for clothing. Deer and elk were rare. Without rabbits, families were defenseless against winter cold. It took one hundred pelts to make a robe for an adult, forty pelts for a child's robe.

Other peoples, such as the Ute, were more fortunate. Where they lived deer, elk, and antelope weren't scarce. Women could use the skins of larger animals as well as rabbit fur to make winter clothing.

By spring, many families had little, if any, food left. Thankfully, the winter rain and snow created marshes. The wetlands attracted ducks, and the people were ready for their arrival.

The men built decoy ducks, using tule to build the "skeleton" of the duck. They attached yucca and cattail leaves to this skeleton to imitate the duck's body. Paint and feathers were added to make the decoy look as real as possible.

The decoys were placed in the water to attract real ducks. Hiding in the reeds, the hunters splashed the water with their fingers to mimic the sound of ducks feeding. The ducks swam toward the familiar sound. As the men hunted the ducks, the women gathered eggs from their nests. The creeks and rivers were full of fish on their way upstream to spawn. Men speared fish. Boys jumped into the water, to catch fish with their bare hands. The abundance of water brought the land to life. Insects, such as grasshoppers, locusts, and ants, were everywhere—and so were women gathering them.

As summer heat increased, the waters dried up. Ducks and fish were harder to find. Fruit, however, was ripening. The land offered people the big-pitted fruit of chokeberries, the pulpy fruit of the yucca, and the prickly fruit of the cactus. Women stewed, dried, or made the fruit into meal. It was also eaten raw. Fruit, if covered in spines, was eaten after the spines were burned off.

Families gathered rice grass in summer. Ute families gathered corn, beans, and squash in fall, and all tribes harvested piñon nuts. But all this could change. A winter with little rain or snow could bring an unhappy spring, and a summer of wind-swept dirt clouding a cloudless sky.

Sparing the Gray Jay

Most Indian peoples didn't hunt all living creatures. The Ute, for example, didn't kill the gray jay. The jay's loud call helped Ute hunters locate the large game they were following.

Healing the Sick Through Song

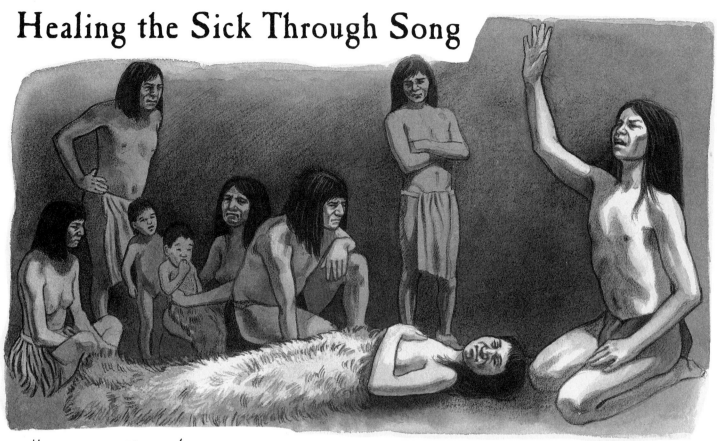

He sang the nine songs.

You have a cold and a fever. You are sick. To the Ute, and all Indian tribes in North America, sickness meant something was out of order—not just in you, but also in the world of spirits that you lived in. The person who made you well, a healer, drew on the power of the spirit world to restore order and your health.

Pa gits was a Ute healer. When he came to a sick person's home he did not bring a rattle. He did not wear a magical mask. He simply brought himself and his invisible spiritual advisor. That was all he needed.

Pa gits first saw his advisor when he was twelve. He was sleeping in the mountains. In his dreams he heard a man singing nine songs. The man was about two feet tall. He was green from head to toe and carried a bow and arrows. Pa gits learned the songs, and then returned home to use the songs to help cure the sick.

When a person was ill, he sent a relative to Pa gits's home carrying the healer's emblem—a forked green stick. Pa gits accepted the emblem. The relative would lead Pa gits to the sick person's home. The spiritual advisor followed.

Pa gits went inside. His advisor remained outside. After talking with the sick person, Pa gits could sense whether his advisor felt they could cure the person's illness. If they felt qualified to cure the person, a two- to three-week treatment began. Every evening, for two hours, Pa gits sang the nine songs his advisor had taught him, before the sick person and his relatives.

If the person's health improved, the healer and his advisor reduced their visits. If his condition got worse they stayed from sunset to sunrise. When the person was finally cured, Pa gits returned home. His advisor returned to his own home, until the time sickness brought them together again.

A SHOSHONI STORY:
THE LITTLE PEOPLE

Many Indian groups throughout North America believed in the existence of Little People or Little Demons. The Shoshoni called them Ninnimbe. A man in Wyoming wrote about the Ninnimbe, based on discussions he had with Indian elders:

"A pioneer in the Wind River country, Wyoming, once came upon several ancient dwellings made of sticks and stones held together with mud, high up in the rocks near the sources of Muddy Creek. Talking about them with a number of Indians, he was told that the structures had been made before the Indians came into the region. They were the homes of Ninnimbe, the Little Demons or Little People. Here are some former beliefs about them.

"The Little People were two or three feet high, strong and fearless. They wore clothing of goatskin and always carried a large quiver [pouch] of arrows on their backs. They were secret stalkers, expert hunters, and good fighters, also, but they sometimes fell prey to eagles. Their poisoned arrows, shot with deadly aim, picked off many of the early Shoshoni. Their arrows were invisible.

"Usually, the Little People themselves were invisible, deep in the woods or in the deep shade of a canyon. But one time a Shoshoni actually saw one of the Ninnimbe. Walking along the edge of a high cliff, the Indian heard a cry like the cry of a child. Looking down, he saw one of the Little People on a ledge, being attacked by an eagle. The Shoshoni climbed down to him and drove the eagle away. The little fellow expressed deep gratitude to the Indian for saving his life. . . .

"One of the Little People is still living. He, too, is called Ninnimbe. Some say that he is a little boy about two feet tall who runs through the mountains, shooting game with his bow and arrows.

"Others say he is an old man, sturdily built, dressed in the skins of mountain sheep that are painted with bright colors. His nose is red. He lives in the mountains, from where he appears and disappears at will. Old stone darts that have been picked up here and there are evidence that he has shot his arrows.

"People do not often call a relative or friend by his true name because of their fear of Ninnimbe. If he should hear anyone's name, he might cause some misfortune to come upon that person, even kill him with his invisible arrows. . . .

"Any misfortune a Shoshoni suffers is due to Ninnimbe. If even a trifling accident occurs when a Shoshoni is starting out on a journey, he will turn back, afraid of Ninnimbe. . . .

"Ninnimbe is always mean, always on the watch for a Shoshoni to do him harm."

The Little People were strong and fearless.

MAKE A MORACHE

Northern Ute musicians played an instrument called a "morache." This instrument had three parts: a notched stick-rattle, a rubbing stick, and a basket resonator.

The basket was placed over a hole in the ground. The musician rested the notched stick-rattle on the basket. The musician rubbed the rubbing stick against the notched stick-rattle.

This created a musical sound. This sound was then conveyed to the basket. The air trapped under the basket began to vibrate as well. You, too, can make a morache.

You Will Need:

An adult to assist you; a hardwood branch, at least 2 feet long and about 1 inch wide; a stubby branch, about 6 inches long and 1 inch wide; a ruler; a saw; sandpaper; a tightly woven basket or a metal bowl; and a trowel.

1. Strip off the bark and any extra branches.
2. Take the 2-foot branch and measure 6 inches from one end of the stick. This 6-inch section will be the instrument's handle.
3. In the remaining 18 inches, you and an adult will cut approximately twenty-seven notches on one side of the branch. The notches are to be about ¾ inch deep.
4. On the other side of the branch, opposite the notched section, measure 12 inches. It should be centered so there are 3 inches of space on either side.
5. In this section cut twenty-four shallow notches. The notches should be no deeper than ⅛ inch.
6. When all the notches have been made, you can smooth any rough edges with sandpaper.
7. Dig a hole in the ground, with your trowel, and cover the hole with your bowl. Or, indoors, place the bowl over a non-carpeted floor.
8. Rest your notched stick-rattle against the bowl.
9. Rub the middle of the rubbing stick against the side with the deeper notches. (You can also rub the rubbing stick against the other side.)

The musical sound you hear was a familiar sound to the Northern Ute.

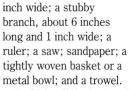

1. Cut extra branches off.

2. 6" for handle

3. Cut 27 notches ¾" deep.

4. 3" 3"

5. Cut 24 notches ⅛" deep.

6.

7A.

7B.

8.

9.

PLAY THE RING-AND-PIN GAME

1.

2.

3. rawhide

4.

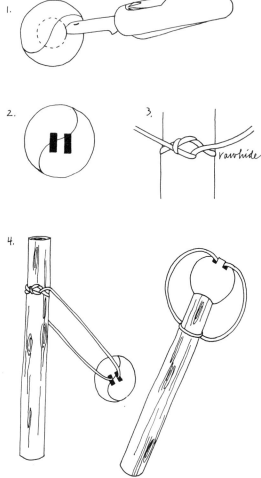

Throughout North America, Indians played a game now known as Ring and Pin. The object of this game was to catch án object on the end of a stick. Today children play the same game trying to catch a ball in a cup.

In the original game, the Indians used a stick about 22 inches long. A length of cord was tied around the stick so that the ends of the cord hung freely.

These two ends were tied to a variety of objects such as a hide ring, a string of bones, and pumpkin rinds. Which object was used depended on what was available. The Paiute used the skulls of small rodents.

You can make a ring and pin, and play the game. Here's how.

You Will Need:

An adult to assist you; a wooden stick about 2 feet long; 2 to 3 feet of rawhide shoestring; a plastic baseball; and a pocketknife.

1. Cut a hole in the baseball, somewhat larger than the width of the stick.
2. Opposite that hole, on the other side of the ball, cut two slits.
3. Tie the middle of the rawhide string around one end of the stick. The string will have two loose ends.
4. Thread one end of the string through the two slits in the ball and tie it to the other end of the rawhide string.

You are ready to catch the ball on the end of the stick. Call over a friend or just play by yourself. Either way it's a challenge.

People of the Plains

A Faraway Rumble

Unable to stop, they plunged over the cliff.

Babies were strapped onto their mothers' backs. Dogs were harnessed to the travois (trav-OY), a frame of two long poles, covered with skins and loaded with household goods. The men walked ahead in small groups, weapons ready, watching, listening. They had begun the summer hunt. Their religious leader, a holy woman, performed rituals that would bring success to the hunters. When they felt the ground tremble, saw the brown cloud of dust on the horizon, and heard the faraway rumble, the people were filled with excitement.

Millions of buffalo roamed the grassy, treeless plains. With its huge, shaggy head, thick shoulder hump, and short legs, this big brown animal looked slow and clumsy. But the people knew better. The animal stood six feet tall and was ten times the weight of a man. Also called the bison, the buffalo was fast and unpredictable. A herd could be grazing aimlessly on grass one minute and suddenly break into a wild stampede. The hunt was deadly dangerous. But for the hunters, the buffalo meant food, clothing, and shelter.

A skilled hunter could kill a buffalo without injuring himself. Though they hunted on foot, the people, who called themselves Absaroka, Children of the Long-beaked Bird—the Crow—had several methods of bringing down their victims.

The Crow usually targeted buffalo that tagged behind the main herd. Two or three hunters would single out a stray and surround it. When it picked up human scent, the buffalo might flee. Just as often, it would turn its massive body, and charge.

But with its poor vision, the buffalo was at a disadvantage. The Crow hid under disguises. Crawling through the dry grass, covered by buffalo or wolf skins and head

masks, the hunters moved closer until they could shoot their bows at close range. To a nearsighted buffalo, these short, furry creatures smelled harmless and even looked about right. When the buffalo realized its mistake, it was too late.

When a Crow village worked together, they could kill several animals at once. One way was to stand the travois poles on end and tie them together to make a rough corral. They called it a pound. The women, children, and dogs stayed at a distance, where their scent wouldn't carry on the wind. The men circled around a small herd, drove it into the pound, and killed their captives.

Sometimes the Crow set a pattern of grass fires. When the frightened buffalo stampeded in the only direction that wasn't burning, a group of men was waiting with their weapons aimed. In rugged areas, like canyons and river gorges, they moved large rocks and lined a wide path leading to the edge of a cliff. Under the cliff, they fenced off a small area. Then they surrounded the herd, driving it forward between the rocks. The buffalo thundered along, straight to the edge. Unable to stop, they plunged over the side. Below the gorge, hunters shot any animals that did not perish in the fall.

As they killed and gathered the buffalo carcasses, the Crow divided the meat and hides evenly between the hunters. They did not kill unnecessarily—only the number they needed for food or skins. For several days they would camp, feasting on fresh roasted buffalo.

The women had hides to clean, horns to scrape, buffalo wool to weave, and meat to dry, or jerk, for the times when the fresh meat was gone.

Using It All

Buffalo were hunted primarily for meat and hides. But the animal's remains were put to many other uses too. The head served as a ceremonial mask for dances or as a disguise worn on a hunt.

Scraped clean, the horns made deep, strong containers to hold things. Buffalo bones made tools for digging and sewing and toys for children to play with. The contents of the gall bladder provided a tonic for illness. Other tough organ skins were cut, stuffed with hair, and tied to make balls and toys for the children.

"A PERSON"

I am a person never absent
from any important act.
Great Elk is the name I have taken.
When men hunt little animals
I will always make them appear
to them.
In the midst of each of the four
winds, I throw myself upon the earth.
I cleanse all the land of my anger.
I throw myself and leave the hairs
of my body—these hairs I have
scattered so that animals may
appear in their midst, they are
the grasses of this earth.
I have made the grasses
so the animals may appear
so you may live
upon the earth
upon the earth.

Osage
(Plains Indian)

LIFE ON THE WIDE, ENDLESS PLAIN

Long ago, the Crow people separated from others who lived farther east and north. They began a journey that took them west. Along the way, they took the name Absaroka, which became "Crow." No longer tied to one land and the corn harvest, they chose a new way of surviving. In their new homeland of endless grassy plains, wide rivers, and deep canyons, hunting was good. They put aside farming and followed herds of elk, deer, and buffalo.

One account in Crow history says that during their travels, they stopped and sought advice from the Great Spirit. A Crow chief fasted and prepared himself for a vision. In a dream, the Great Spirit gave him a sacred tobacco seed and told him to make a long journey to the place of the big mountain. There his people should plant the tobacco seed. It was not to be smoked, but kept for its seed. It would be a good land, and the people, small in number, would do well.

Their journey took them in many directions. They went north, but found it snowy and cold. They went south again, and then west. Finally, they came back to a place where two great rivers meet. Today these rivers are called the Missouri and the Yellowstone. A little farther west, the travelers came to the Bighorn Mountains, where they planted the tobacco seed. They stayed in the land near the rivers, and became known as the River Crow. As the Great Spirit had promised, their lives were good.

Later some of the River Crow separated again, and moved even farther west. They became known as the Mountain Crow. But both groups gathered together often, and always thought of themselves as one people.

Tobacco
Plant

She covered the outside of the poles with buffalo skins.

FOLLOWING THE HERD IN THEIR "MOBILE" HOMES

When the Crow stopped to build their camps, women did the work of setting up the shelter, the tipi, and getting it in order. What a relief for the family dog to be unhitched from its heavy harness. The long travois poles it dragged had another important use: they became poles to support the cone-shaped tipi, or lodge, the woman was about to assemble.

The size of her tipi depended on her family's wealth. Some were very large. The Crow woman made a wide circle of the long slender poles, angling them so they met at the top. She spread a layer of buffalo skins on the ground inside the circle and she covered the outside of the poles with others.

Where the tipi poles met at the top, two flaps could be opened when they were needed to break the winds sweeping over the Plains. They also worked as a chimney. The woman built a fire on the floor in the center of the tipi. With the flaps opened, the smoke went straight up and out the top.

The tipi was set up with the door facing east. The Crow believed that the east was the source of both light and knowledge. At dawn, they stepped out to light a sacred pipe or offer a morning prayer.

Inside it was comfortable. Beds of buffalo skins lined the outside walls. Hanging between two tipi poles was a tanned hide—a clean, smooth buffalo skin that had been painted to tell the family's history. When there was a special dance, the hide was taken down and worn as a robe.

The woman stored her family's belongings in several leather bags and pouches that hung from *tripods*—three sticks set up to lean against each other. They were held in place by leather thongs wrapped at the top. Inside the bags and pouches she kept extra clothes, scraps of leather for making moccasins, her paints, brushes made of buffalo bone, her porcupine-quill comb, and sewing materials. Some of the storage bags were decorated with beautiful porcupine quill-work dyed in bright colors.

Buffalo skins that covered the tipi had to be free of holes. During a rainstorm, drops pelted the lodge with a soft, soothing sound. When deep snow piled up around the outside of the tipi, the hides were good insulation, holding in the heat from the fire.

Fighting for Survival

Tall, muscular, with high cheekbones and straight dark hair, the Crow became exceptional hunters. Outnumbered by other people living on the Plains, many times they had to defend their buffalo hunting grounds against enemies.

The Crow lived with danger. Their survival required them to keep a constant watch for trouble. When it came, they fought back with superior skill.

Make a Tipi

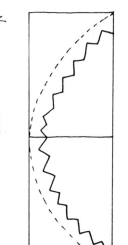

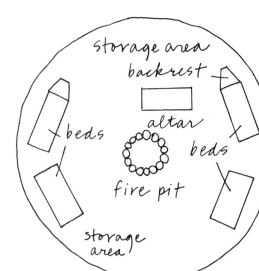

Some people—not just American Indians—still build and live in tipis today. If they are built carefully, with the proper materials, tipis are works of art.

You can make your *own* tipi. There are books that have detailed instructions for building an authentic tipi of natural materials or canvas. But for a dwelling you just want to play in, these instructions will do the job. Ask a grownup or a friend to help you set it up.

Add any finishing touches you wish, like exterior decorations, a round hole for the entrance, even a window with a flap if you want one. Your tipi will be a great hideout when you want to be alone, a nice place to sleep, and a good place to play with your friends.

What You Need:

Two old bedsheets; one or two old blankets; six to ten wooden, plastic, or bamboo poles that measure between 5 and 7 feet tall (the larger your sheets are and the taller your poles, the bigger you can make your tipi); a 4-foot piece of sturdy rope or twine; several large safety pins; a needle and some heavy-duty thread (or a sewing machine and a grownup to help you run it); waterproof spray (if you want to keep your tipi outside).

1. Match and pin the short ends of the sheets together, and sew them by hand or machine.

2. Using the illustration as a guide, cut the sheet to make a large half circle. *Note:* Hemming the raw edges is not necessary, but it will give the tipi a finished look and prevent the raw edges from fraying.

3. Stand the poles up two or three at a time, spreading them to form a wide circle. Lash them together with the twine, weaving it over, under, and around them to hold them in place.

4. Drape the tipi covering over the poles. Pin it in place at the top, and pin or sew it by hand from the top to about 18 inches from the bottom ends.

5. For the entrance, pin back the flaps where you left the second seam open, or pin or stitch the seam all the way to the bottom, and cut out a circular doorway near the bottom, cutting through the seam.

6. Spread an old blanket or two on the inside and smooth out the wrinkles in them.

sewing line

storage area

backrest

altar

beds

beds

fire pit

storage area

door faces east

Interior of the Plains Indians Tipis

LITTLE GIRLS HUNTED BUFFALO TOO

Pretty-shield was a Mountain Crow girl. Her grandfather named her on the fourth day of her life. She lived in what is now southeastern Montana, moving across the great land, following the buffalo. We do not know exactly when she was born, but we think it must have been around 1860. Pretty-shield was the fourth child in her family of eleven brothers and sisters, but she grew up among the River Crow, with her aunt, Strikes-with-an-axe.

Not long after Pretty-shield was born, Strikes-with-an-axe's two little girls had died. They were killed by an enemy tribe. Pretty-shield was sent to comfort her aunt, and stayed to live with her. The little girl liked living in her aunt's big lodge. She did not feel far away from her own family because the Crow people traveled constantly and met often.

Pretty-shield loved moving. It was an adventure, and a time to see her mother and sisters again. These are her own words about moving:

"The great herds of buffalo were constantly moving, and of course we moved when they did. I never tired of moving. . . . I carried my doll on my back just as mothers carry their babies; and besides this I had a little tepee [tipi] that I pitched whenever my aunt pitched hers. It was made exactly like my aunt's, had the same number of poles, only of course my tepee was very small. My horse dragged the poles and packed the lodge-skin [tipi covering], so that I often beat my aunt in setting up my lodge. . . . And how I used to hurry in setting up my lodge, so that I might have a fire going inside it before my aunt could kindle one in hers! I did not know it then, but now I feel sure that she often let me beat her just to encourage me.

"Each year, as was our custom, I made myself a new lodge and set it up, as the grownups did, when we went into our winter camps. Each time . . . I cut my lodge-skin larger than the old one, took more and more pains to have it pretty. I played with these little lodges, often lived in them, until I was a married woman, and even after. I have never lost my love for play."

One of the experiences Pretty-shield remembered best was the day she and her friends decided to make their playing more *real*.

"Once several of us girls made ourselves a play-village with our tiny tepees. Of course our children were dolls, and our horses dogs, and yet we . . . made our village look very real, so real that we thought we ought to have some meat to cook. We decided to kill it ourselves. A girl named Beaver-that-passes and I said we would be the hunters, that we would go out to a buffalo herd that was in sight and kill a calf [a baby buffalo].

"Knowing that we could not handle a bow, Beaver-that-passes borrowed her father's lance [long spear] that was very sharp, and longer than both our bodies put together. We caught and saddled two gentle packhorses. . . . I helped all I could, but it was Beaver-that-passes who wounded a big calf that gave us both a lot of trouble before we finally got it down, and dead. I hurt my leg, and Beaver-that-passes cut her hand with the lance. The calf itself looked pretty bad by the time we got it to our play-village. But we had a big feast, and forgot our hurts."

When Pretty-shield's mother heard about this, like *any* mother, she had something to say to her mischievous daughter.

"'You and your friend, Beaver-that-passes, will come to a bad end if you keep doing these crazy things,'" her mother warned.

Beaver-that-passes wounded a big calf.

Grab Your Toys and Run

Straight to the lodge she raced, determined to save her toys.

Pretty-shield's favorite toys were her little doll and her ball. She took them both almost everywhere she went. She carried her doll on her back, tucked into her buffalo robe. Her older sister made the ball for her, from the outer skin of a buffalo heart. It was stuffed with antelope hair and painted red and blue.

One day Pretty-shield left her toys at her little lodge in camp. She and her friends decided to go to the edge of a cliff near the river. They pretended to have a Sun Dance. One boy beat the drum and another danced with the girls. They all blew whistles made from eagle bones. Dancing to the drum with their eyes on the sky, the children forgot everything around them.

Suddenly one of the boys stopped. An enemy war party stared down at them from the cliff above. For a few moments, the children froze with fear, unable to move.

Then, racing as fast as they could, they scrambled down the hill to their parents. Arrows were already flying as Pretty-shield remembered her toys.

She heard her aunt call, but she did not stop. Straight to her lodge she raced, determined to save her toys from the enemy. As she ran through camp, an old Crow woman caught her and promised to hide the toys for her.

When Pretty-shield returned to the old woman's lodge to get her toys, her doll was safe, but the ball was ruined. It had rolled into a creek and was soaked. Sadly, Pretty-shield carried it home and showed her aunt.

Strikes-with-an-axe knew what to do. Pretty-shield watched as she cut the sinew and pulled out the dirty wet stuffing. Packed with a fistful of fresh horsehair and wiped clean, the ball looked and felt as good as new.

But the day ended in tragedy. The warriors were driven away, but when the Crow men returned, the village was gripped in sorrow. A young warrior, the father of one of Pretty-shield's friends, had been killed.

The Old Mother Bear

Pretty-shield was usually good. But her mother was right; there was no denying that she found life full of adventure. One summer day she and her friends were playing in a pine tree when some Crow boys came along. They had roped a mother white (grizzly) bear and her two cubs.

The boys dragged the growling bears over to the tree, teasing the girls, "Come down and play with our little pets."

Pretty-shield could see that the old mother bear was missing almost all her teeth and her claws were so worn down that she wasn't dangerous. Pretty-shield knew the mother would not try to climb the tree. She knew, too, that if *she* climbed down and raced home, she could make it. But she was afraid to try.

Finally the boys went back to camp and told her father what they had done. He came to the tree, laughing. "Come down," he said, "that old bear has no teeth to bite anything." Her father and the two boys untied the mother grizzly and one cub and let them go. They took the other cub back to the village and gave it to Pretty-shield's aunt, who kept it as a pet for two years.

Pretty-shield's Calendar

Pretty-shield's bear adventure happened in the summer. She didn't say "June," as we would today. She remembered it "in the moon when the leaves are fully grown."

Pretty-shield was born in March, "in the moon when ice goes out of the rivers." April was "the moon when the sage-hens dance." July was "the moon when the berries turn red." September was "the moon that plums fall." November was "the moon when leaves are on the ground."

Calendars weren't necessary to most Indian cultures. When they were, the people found different ways of marking the path of the sun across the land, or counting the phases of the moon. Of course, their lives changed constantly, according to the weather and the seasons—when it was time to plant, to hunt, to hold ceremonies, to settle for the winter.

Think of the past year in your life, starting with "the moon of your birthday." If you didn't have a calendar, could you recall a special event that would help you remember each "moon" of the year?

Pretty-shield knew the mother would not try to climb the tree.

Make a Pair of Moccasins

Leather moccasins were worn by most Indian tribes in America. Each had its own traditional style, and each decorated them, especially for ceremonies, with beads and feathers.

Perhaps you never thought you could make your own "shoes," but it's not difficult. Suede moccasins are warm and comfortable for wearing in the house. (They aren't recommended for outdoor wear.)

The style shown here is a simple, one-piece pattern, which has only two seams. Before you make it in suede, however, make a paper pattern and practice on a model pair made from fabric scraps or denim—your old blue jeans would be great for this. (If you're lucky, your moccasins will fit the first time around.) Have a grownup handy in case you need help.

You Will Need:

A piece of denim or another sturdy fabric, sharp scissors, chalk or a marker, a needle, and some heavy-duty thread, lightweight suede, small leather hole punch, a needle, and some waxed nylon thread. (Leather shops carry these materials.)

1. With a dark marker, trace the sole of one of your feet as you stand on newspaper. Following the shape in the illustration, enlarge the pattern, adding 1½ inches around the heel and toe areas and almost double the size of your foot to each side. (You can always stitch and trim your moccasins smaller, but once the fabric is cut, you can't make them larger.)

2. Cut out the newspaper pattern. Lay the pattern on the denim and trace around it with light chalk or a marker.

3. Cut out the fabric. Fold it in half with the tops together and the good sides of the fabric on the inside.

4. Thread the needle with a strand of heavy-duty thread, knotted at the ends to make it double. Using a ¼-inch running stitch, sew the toe section together, beginning where the top cuff makes a corner with the top foot section and ending at the toe fold (see illustration). Take several tiny stitches at the toe to lock the thread.

5. Using another double strand of thread knotted at the ends, stitch the heel piece from cuff to foot, ending with several lock stitches.

6. Turn the moccasin right-side out and try it on. Adjust the fit. If it's very large, sew new seams inside the old ones. If it's too small, enlarge the

newspaper pattern and cut another pattern and model. Draw your other foot now. Cut out the pattern and sew your second moccasin.

7. When the moccasins fit right, begin the suede pair. Fold the suede with the brushed sides together on the inside and lay the pattern on the folded suede. Trace around the pattern and cut out the suede pieces.

8. Using the small leather hole punch, punch holes ¼ inch apart and ½ inch in from the edge of the suede, as shown in the illustration. Punch the top foot section and the heel section. Repeat with the other moccasin.

9. Fold one moccasin together, brushed side on the inside, with tops matching. Match the punched holes together as closely as possible and lace the moccasin together, using waxed nylon thread. Beginning where you did with the denim model, stick the needle down into two matched holes, through the suede, and up into the next two matched holes. Continue stitching until the top foot section is sewn. Tie a very tight knot in the waxed nylon thread. Snip the thread, leaving a 1-inch tail. Sew the heel section and knot as before. Sew the other moccasin.

10. *With a grownup's supervision*, wave a lighted match close enough to the knot to barely melt and seal it. Avoid touching the match directly on the knot or it will burn away. While the knot is warm, press it flat and trim the tail. *Suggestion: Practice on scrap knots until you can melt them without melting through the rest of the thread.*

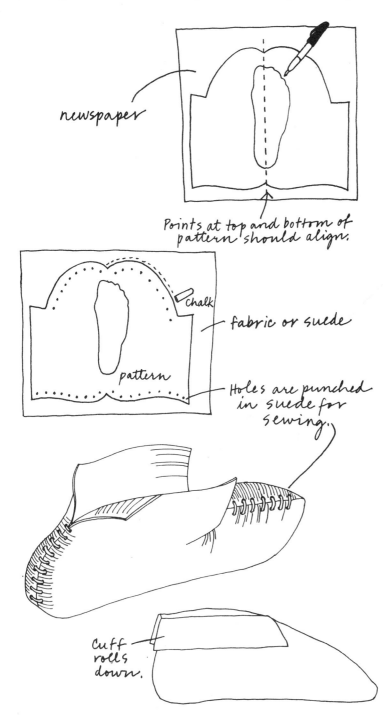

newspaper

Points at top and bottom of pattern should align.

chalk

fabric or suede

pattern

Holes are punched in suede for sewing.

Cuff rolls down.

THE ANIMAL THAT CHANGED LIVES

The Crow people arrived in the land of the Bighorn Mountains about four hundred years ago, around A.D. 1600. About the same time, something else appeared on the land and changed the lifeways of nearly all the Indians in North America.

It was the horse. The horse was brought to North America on ships from Spain. Spanish invaders rode their horses north from Mexico into the Southwest on explorations.

The Indians saw the great advantage of having horses, and little by little began to trade for them or to take them in raids. Southern tribes traded them to their eastern and northern neighbors. In time, horses were common almost everywhere.

Because horses were so valued they became a mark of a person's wealth. Raiders who were successful at stealing horses were honored for their skill, courage, and stealth. A good steed was a treasured possession.

The Indians began breeding their new horses to develop a stronger animal. The Spanish horse, half Andalusian and half Arabian, gradually evolved into the small Indian pony with its shaggy coat. It did not need the rich mixture of grains a larger horse required. The pony could survive on the short wild grasses of the Plains.

What it lacked in physical beauty it more than made up for in speed and intelligence. The Indian pony was superior to any other horse on the Plains. It could pull more weight than the dog. The lodge poles it dragged could be longer, so tipis became larger.

In some languages, the Indian word for pony meant "large dog." In a short time, however, the pony came to be of much greater importance in a spiritual sense. In a hunt or in a battle, the Indian and his pony thought and moved as one. Many times it was the prize in a successful battle against an enemy.

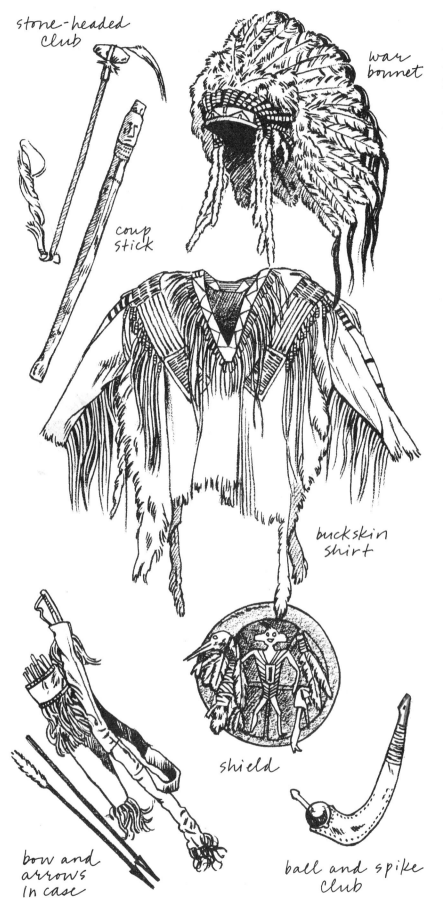

stone-headed club

coup stick

war bonnet

buckskin shirt

shield

bow and arrows in case

ball and spike club

DRESSED TO KILL

Every Crow warrior made weapons and clothing for battle. To the last symbol, the war costume told tales of bravery and warned enemies of astounding ability.

Headdress: The chief wore a full-length "war bonnet" of golden eagle feathers. Made of two hundred or more eagle feathers, they were attached to a headcovering of fur or hair. Mounted at either side were buffalo horns, rubbed with dye and polished to a shine. Long clusters of feathers, quills, and animal furs might also hang from the war bonnet.

Buffalo shirt: During the colder months, the warrior fought in a buffalo or deerskin shirt, decorated with porcupine quills and feathers, and fringes on the sleeves, sometimes made of human scalps. The sides of his leggings were painted and sewn with bands of bright quills too.

Shield: The shield of the warrior was made from a stiff, round piece of buffalo leather. Like his painted pony, his shield told the story of battles he won, coups he earned, horses he captured, and men he killed.

Coup stick: The warrior rode with a long coup stick. He tied the pole with fur tassels and one eagle feather for each scalp he had taken in battle. He also decorated it with other symbols of his power.

Arrows: The warrior chipped different kinds of arrow points for different purposes. One of the most deadly was shaped with a wide point and deep sides that penetrated flesh and was difficult to remove. For war, points were often wrapped loosely to the shaft. When they were shot, the tip entered the flesh, but the shaft fell away. Without its shaft, an arrow point was very difficult to extract.

PAINTED PONIES

The warrior shared his horse with no one. He rode it proudly. Before a battle, when he finished painting himself, he painted his horse. The designs he marked on his war pony and the colors he used were history lessons about both pony and rider.

Symbols painted in blue referred to wounds. Red, for bloodshed, meant courage and bravery. White clay stripes painted under the pony's eyes or on its flanks told how many horses the fighter had captured.

"Keyhole" shape: medicine. This tells that the rider has some kind of medicine power.

A square "U" along the neck: hoofprints. They tell of successful horse raids.

Teardrops: mourning. A warrior who lost a brother, wife, or other special person would ride into battle to honor the person's memory.

Handprint on the flank: combat. The rider killed an enemy in hand-to-hand fighting.

Horizontal stripes: "coup" marks. *Coup* (KU) is a French word meaning a hit or blow. The Plains Indians earned coups when they disgraced their enemy by touching him at close range. There were four main ways to earn coups: strike the enemy with a weapon, capture his horse, get his weapon, or ride him down in battle. Agile young warriors—faster and more daring than their elders—sometimes could make coups using a feather. The more coups the warrior counted, the braver he was thought to be.

With coup lines painted on his pony, both warrior and horse commanded respect. The proud warrior shared every honor with his war horse.

Before a fight, it was customary for the warrior to speak solemnly to his horse. He might use words like these: "We face danger here. Obey me promptly that we may conquer. If you must, run for your life and mine. Do your best. If we reach home, I will give you the best eagle feather I can get, and you shall be painted with the best paint."

OTHER INDIAN SYMBOLS

Bear Tracks — Ancient Bird — Antelope

Blanket — Deer — Talk

Bow & Arrow — Beaver Tail — Bird Tracks

Arrows — Bad

What *Is* Medicine?

The medicine the Indians used wasn't aspirin. It wasn't something they took to cure an illness. In tribal societies, medicine means the spiritual power or help that people receive from nature. This power, usually just called medicine, may be a special trait associated with an animal or natural object. Bird medicine, for example, could bring the person unusually sharp vision and swiftness.

When a person has a vision—an experience of the mind or soul—he or she is usually in a dreamlike state. Supernatural visions and illusions may appear with an intensity that makes them seem real. Sometimes the form of an animal appears and explains how the new power should be used.

A person who receives medicine or a vision knows that it is a rare gift, meant to be used properly. It is understood that careless use of medicine can bring harm.

The warrior shared every honor with his war horse.

The Sun Dance

The most important ceremony among the Crow people was the Sun Dance. It was held on the high plains during a full moon in late summer. The dance varied from one tribe to another, but for all the Plains Indians, some aspects of it were the same. It was a celebration of nature and a time to gather spiritual (medicine) power. Most of all, those who took part in it received power they could use over their enemies.

The Sun Dance did not happen every year. It was called, or pledged, after someone received a vision that guided him or her to prepare for it. The vision came to a person who had lost a relative or close companion at the hands of enemies. During the Sun Dance, the grieving seeker hoped to receive power for revenge against those enemies. Outnumbered by other unfriendly tribes on the Plains, the Crow placed great emphasis on the Sun Dance.

Sometimes the dancers pledged themselves to the Sun Dance for years before it took place. They spent a year preparing themselves, fasting, seeking visions to help them, smoking the sacred pipe for physical and spiritual purity, and behaving according to a strict code. Warriors were not the only people who participated in the Sun Dance. Ordinary men and some women received a vision telling them to pledge the ceremony. They told the chief of their pledge, and the people of the village helped with preparations for the twelve-day dance.

The lodge for the Sun Dance was built several weeks ahead. The Crow went into the mountains to pray before they cut the twenty-four trees that would become the lodge poles. A cottonwood tree was chosen for the center pole, surrounded by a circle of pines. Songs, smoke from the sacred pipe, and brushing with eagle feathers changed the trees' purpose as they became part of the ritual, joining the people to the powers of the universe.

Fires were lighted inside and outside the lodge and were kept burning until the dancing and vision were completed. The people gathered and set up their tipis around the lodge, leaving the east side free. The east represented (and still does) the source of light and knowl-

edge. Nothing must block the sun's path from the sky to the big lodge.

Many rituals of the Sun Dance were completed during the preparations. The person who pledged the dance fasted and prayed for a vision. During eight days of preparation before the dance, the pledger led the people on four hunts to collect only buffalo tongues and the best meat. In a drama that symbolized the return of warriors after a battle, the buffalo meat was given to the twenty bravest warriors.

The number four was repeated over and over, in songs and smoke purifications, while the face and body of the pledger were painted with white clay, to represent a buffalo wallowing in the earth. Later in the ceremony, eight warriors entered the lodge and told of their war deeds. Drumming, rattles, and war cries filled the lodge, as the warriors' might was transferred to the pledger.

On the eighth day of the Sun Dance, the pledger began his full fast and his dancing. His body was painted again with white clay, and a bed of cedar boughs and buffalo skins was made

for him inside the lodge. Buffalo tongues were cooked in the fire in the middle of the lodge. Young warriors, wives, and relatives brought weapons taken from enemies and piled them on the floor. Sometimes the pledger had his flesh pierced and tied with rawhide ropes that hung from the lodge poles.

During that day and the next, he alternated between dancing and listening to warriors recite coup stories. His ceremonial guide chose medicine-songs to sing to him, and placed a medicine bundle before him.

When the vision occurred, the dancer lost his balance and fell. The guide helped him to the bed and covered him with robes. The dance was over. The gathered spectators left in groups, until only the family remained. When he felt revived, they helped the exhausted dancer to his own tipi.

In a few days, the camp would move on. The lodge was left standing. In the year to come, when they met the enemy, the people would know if the vision was good.

The Ant People

When she was thirteen, Pretty-shield's father promised her in marriage to a Crow warrior named Goes-ahead. Now that she was becoming a woman, Pretty-shield tried harder to act grown-up. Three years later, she and Goes-ahead were married. Goes-ahead was brave and kind. Pretty-shield won the honor of painting her own face when he went into battle. Sometimes she was allowed to carry his shield.

Goes-ahead was a good hunter. He shared meat with Pretty-shield's family. She cleaned the hides from the animals he killed, and kept their lodge neat. Pretty-shield was proud of her life as a Crow woman.

Soon Pretty-shield knew that she was going to have a child. In Crow families, all the women cared for the children. Pretty-shield's sisters would help her with the new baby. It was a girl. But the baby was not healthy, and no one could make it well. Pretty-shield was filled with deep sorrow when it died.

For two moons after her baby died, the young mother lived inside a darkness that would not heal. She could not eat. She could not sleep. Day by day she grew weaker, hoping for a medicine-dream to show her how to live.

Pretty-shield left the camp. For three nights she slept among the rocks on a high cliff. The night air was cold. Pretty-shield stayed awake, watching the sky and the stars, and listening to the wind.

On the fourth morning, she returned to camp. Ahead of her, a woman was hurrying toward Pretty-shield's lodge. Suddenly the woman was standing beside an ant hill. She turned and called out, "Come here, Daughter."

The woman told Pretty-shield to rake up the edges of the ant hill and, as she was doing this, to ask for the things she needed. Pretty-shield did what the woman had said.

The woman disappeared. The wind began to blow and Pretty-shield entered a beautiful white lodge. In the brightness, an eagle swept down before her. Pretty-shield saw that it was a war eagle. As quickly as it appeared, the eagle and the white lodge vanished.

Trembling, Pretty-shield found that she was alone again near her own lodge. She sat in the silence for a long time, seeing her medicine-dream. At once she began to feel its power.

The ant people were Pretty-shield's medicine. She turned to them for help, and listened to them. For her, they were "busy, powerful little people, the ants." The people, too, knew that she had received this vision on the mountain. She became a Crow medicine woman.

People of the Northeast

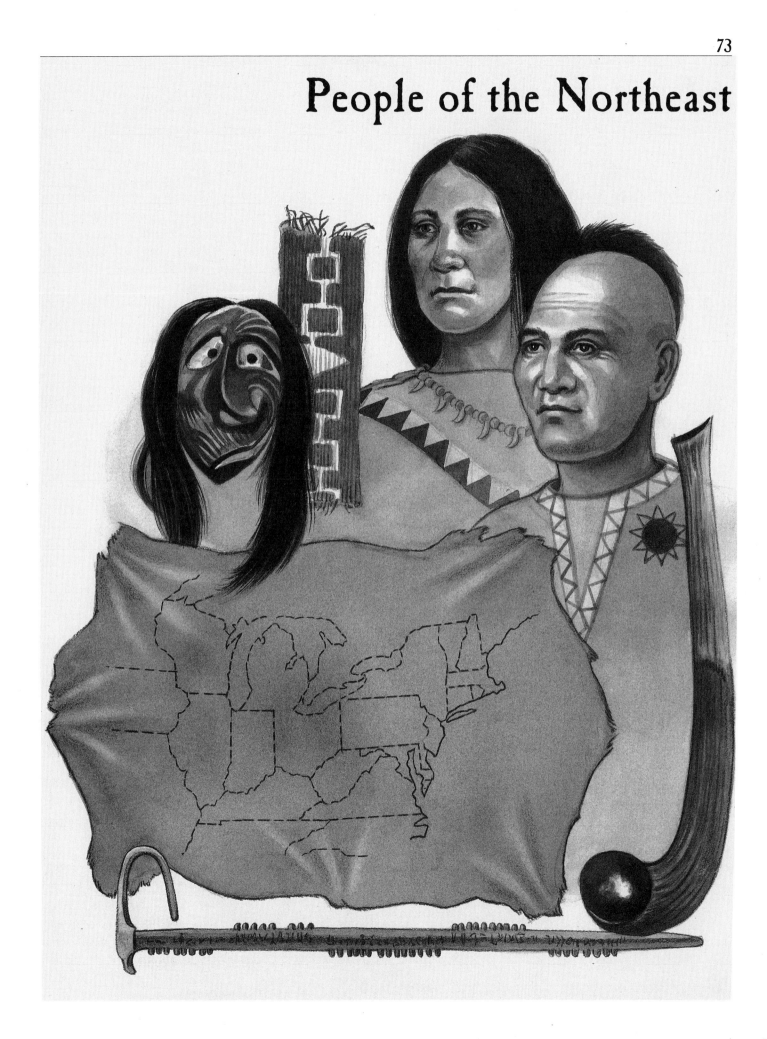

A Circle of Peace

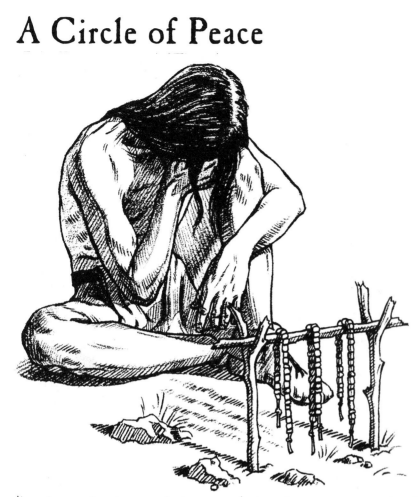

He draped three strings of beads over a stick.

Tadodaho, the leader of the Onondaga nation, was feared by everyone, including his own people. Tadodaho had magical powers. His body had seven crooks. His hands were like the claws of a turtle, and an evil mind lived beneath his hair of serpents. His people were constantly at war with the neighboring peoples: the Seneca, the Cayuga, the Oneida, and the Mohawk, who were also at war with each other.

Among the Onondaga lived a man named Hayenwatha, more commonly spelled "Hiawatha." He was determined to end the blood feuds that kept his people constantly at war. Hayenwatha requested a council with Tadodaho and his council members. He tried to persuade them to embrace peace, not war. Tadodaho refused. The council members also refused. To defy their chief meant certain death.

Not long after the council ended, Hayenwatha's eldest daughter fell ill and died. Her illness was sudden. Her sickness could not be cured. Many believed Tadodaho's evil power caused this tragedy.

Hayenwatha was deeply saddened by his daughter's death, but it didn't discourage him. He called for another council. It too was a failure. Once again, Hayenwatha was punished for his courageous efforts. His second daughter became ill and died, in the same way his eldest daughter had been stricken.

After mourning the death of his second daughter, Hayenwatha asked for a third council. His youngest daughter came with him. As the council started, his daughter went with the other women to collect firewood.

An eagle appeared in the sky. Seeing the eagle, Tadodaho ordered his finest warrior to kill the bird. The warrior fired an arrow and killed the eagle in flight.

The eagle fell to the ground. The warriors rushed to the eagle to pluck its prized feathers. In their haste, they ran over Hayenwatha's youngest daughter, trampling her to death.

Hayenwatha was overcome with grief. He left the Onondaga village and wandered the land. He was alone with his sorrow and no one could comfort him.

He stopped and made three strings of beads out of rushes. He took two forked sticks and pushed them into the ground. Hayenwatha rested a stick across the forks and draped the three strings of beads over this stick. And he said, "This would I do if I found anyone burdened with grief even as I am. I would console them for they would be covered with night and wrapped in darkness. This would I lift with words of condolence and these strings of beads would become words with which I would address them."

Hayenwatha stood up and continued on. He came upon a group of small lakes. He had entered the land where the Mohawk lived. He strung a string of white shells, a symbol of peace, and sat down.

A young woman came upon him. She returned to the village and told the others of a man holding a string of white shells. Dekanawidah, a holy man, was living in the village. He believed that all men were brothers and that the killing must stop.

Dekanawidah asked that this man be invited into the village. The holy man listened to Hayenwatha's painful story, and how he suffered trying to stop the endless fighting. He realized Hayenwatha wanted peace as much as he did.

Together, Hayenwatha and the holy man

Dekanawidah began singing.

worked to bring about the Great Peace, Kayanernh-kowa. They began with the Mohawk. They were the first to embrace the Great Peace. The Oneida, the Cayuga, and many of the Seneca followed. The Onondaga wanted peace; their leader, Tadodaho, did not.

Dekanawidah, Hayenwatha, and a delegation of chiefs set out to convince the wicked Tadodaho to accept the Great Peace.

They traveled to his village. Dekanawidah began singing. He told Tadodaho the song he was singing was Tadodaho's song and his alone. It was called "I use it to beautify the earth."

Seeing that the chief's hate was fading, Dekanawidah passed his hands over Tadodaho's turtle-shaped feet. His feet became like those of men. The holy man changed the chief's hideous hands and his hair of serpents. Finally he straightened the chief's crooked body. The wickedness that had distorted Tadodaho's body had been removed, and with it his desire for war.

He was told that the delegation of chiefs agreed to make him the leading chief of this new united council. Tadodaho accepted.

Hayenwatha and Dekanawidah brought together the chiefs of the five tribes. They gathered in the land of the Onondaga and formed the first peace council, called the Great Council.

Dekanawidah planted the Great Tree of Peace. Around a Great Council Fire, the leaders agreed to form a partnership ruled by a government of laws. The blood feuds were over. A union known as the Five Nations, or the Iroquois Nation, had begun. The leaders formed a circle.

These words were said, "We bind ourselves together by taking hold of each other's hands so firmly, and forming a circle so strong that if a tree should fall upon it, it could not shake nor break it, so that our people and grandchildren shall remain in the circle in security, peace, and happiness."

Out of war had come a circle of peace.

One Story, Many Stories

The story of how the Iroquois League was formed has been passed on for over five hundred years. It was not read from a book, but told and retold in villages. Stories differed between villages. The story you have read is just one version of what happened.

He gave Hayenwatha the first string.

THE THREE WORDS OF CONDOLENCE

When Hayenwatha met Dekanawidah he had the three strings of beads he had made to comfort himself. Dekanawidah later picked up these same strings one at a time. He gave Hayenwatha the first string and said, "When a person has suffered a great loss caused by death and is grieving, the tears blind his eyes so that he cannot see. With these words, I wipe away the tears from your eyes so that now you may see clearly."

The holy man gave Hayenwatha the second string and said, "When a person has suffered a great loss caused by death and is grieving, there is an obstruction in his ears and he cannot hear. With these words I remove the obstruction from your ears so that you may once again have perfect hearing."

Dekanawidah gave Hayenwatha the third string and said, "When a person has suffered a great loss caused by death, his throat is stopped and he cannot speak. With these words, I remove the obstruction from your throat so that you may speak and breathe freely."

These are the "three words" of the Condolence Ceremony. The ceremony is still conducted today.

THE GREAT COUNCIL GATHERED

A slender stream of smoke rose from a hill into the chilly fall air. The Great Council Fire was burning. It was a signal to the peoples that the Great Council of the Five Nations was in session.

The councilors, or chiefs, talked among themselves waiting for the opening ceremony to begin. They talked of their summer, children, and war. War still existed. The individual groups of the Five Nations didn't battle each other any longer. The Iroquois Nation, however, as one single "army" continued to do battle against neighboring enemies.

The councilors also talked about the recent death of one of the Mohawk councilors as they smoked from a long cane pipe—and of the new councilor who was sent to replace him. The Mohawk elder women, or matrons, had chosen the replacement. Women chose all the chiefs of the Great Council. The chiefs followed the wishes of the elder women, but no women were allowed to sit on the council.

The men greeted the new councilor, using his personal name given to him by his mother. It would be the first and last time the new councilor would hear his name at the Great Council. After the opening ceremony he would, for the rest of his life, be called by the name of the chief who first held his council seat.

Now, the opening ceremony, the Condolence Ceremony, began. The Onondaga speaker stated to the Great Council that their forefathers had created this nation. He told them that their forefathers, the fifty original chiefs, must be called out to guarantee that the nation continued.

The speaker brought forth a cane, made of sugar maple. On the cane were inscribed the clans of the five peoples and pegs that stood for the original fifty-member council.

One by one he solemnly began the roll call of the chiefs, starting with the Mohawk chiefs. Every so often various seated chiefs called out, "Hai, Hai." This was the cry of the souls. If these cries were not made, it would anger the departed souls. They would send disease down upon the people.

The speaker continued the roll call, making sure that before he stated each chief's name, he said, "Continue to listen, you who were a ruler." After he finished calling out the Mohawk chiefs, he said, "This was the roll of you. You

A Mohawk counselor rose and gave an emotional speech.

that joined in the work. You who completed the work. The Great League." He would make this statement after naming each of the five groups of chiefs.

The chief who had recently died was also mourned at this time. A chief was like a tree. When he died, it was like a tree being uprooted. Now it was time to "raise up" or plant a new tree, a new chief. The new chief, or councilor, was formally introduced.

The next day, a fire was made and all the councilors were sworn in. The Onondaga chiefs cleaned the area around the fire. The Onondaga speaker held the five wampum strings, which represented the five tribes, in his hand and called for the Great Council meeting to begin.

The issue before the council was announced: Should the Iroquois Nation seek to go to battle against an Algonquin village for killing members of a Mohawk hunting party?

A Mohawk councilor rose and gave an emotional speech describing the violent acts of the Algonquin warriors against the Mohawk hunters. He mentioned the location of the Algonquin village and made it clear that the hunters weren't trespassing. The new Mohawk councilor listened. Someday he would have to stand before the council and speak, asking for their agreement.

When the speaker finished, the Mohawk councilors divided into three groups to discuss what the speaker had said. Two groups took part in the discussion. One group listened to make sure no one had misunderstood what the Mohawk speaker had said.

When the Mohawk chiefs had come to an agreement, they gave their opinion to the Seneca councilors. When both the Mohawk and Seneca councilors agreed, their opinion was passed across the fire to the Cayuga and Oneida councilors. When they reached agreement, the decision was sent across the fire to the Onondaga councilors for their approval.

If they agreed with the others, the council's decision would be announced in the name of the Iroquois Nation. If they didn't, the discussion was started all over again starting with the Mohawk chiefs. Getting everyone to agree took time. A decision could be reached in days, but then again, it could take weeks, or even longer.

This time, the Great Council took three weeks to make their decision. Eventually, everyone agreed not to attack the Algonquin village. It was located too near a Mohawk village. The possibility of this Mohawk village being attacked was too great. The safest battles were those waged far from home.

The business of the Great Council was finished. The Onondaga speaker once again held the wampum strings in his hand and called the meeting closed. The chiefs returned to their villages. The smoke that rose up from the hill for days would rise no more till the council met again next fall.

Ruled by Women

Iroquois men owned their clothing, personal possessions, and weapons. In the world beyond the village, men hunted and waged war.

Women owned everything else. They also controlled life within the village. Women were responsible for growing crops, managing the stored foods, and supervising the men during the harvest.

And even though they couldn't go to war, controlling food production allowed women to control whether a war began or not.

If the women chose to discourage a war, they simply refused to give the warriors their moccasins and to fill their bearskin food bags with cornmeal laced with maple syrup. Without food and footwear there could be no war.

If Only Summer Could Last Forever

She bangs the mallet against the gourd.

Light streams in through the square smoke holes of the longhouse roof. Sun falls on the girl's face, waking her. She sits up on the sleeping platform that is lined with bearskins. Her mother and two brothers are still asleep, but not for long.

Her father and many of the men are not in the village. They are hunting and will not return for three days. The men are often away. If they aren't hunting, they are trading with villages, or taking part in raids. However, not every man goes. A group of young warriors always remains behind to guard the village.

The girl stands up, smoothing out her deerskin skirt, and slips into her moccasins. She gives thanks for being alive. She yawns and stretches her hands toward the high-arched ceiling where herbs and roots hang from the rafters drying. The girl looks down the hundred-foot corridor of the longhouse, blanketed in a thin veil of smoke from a fire. Two families are eating by this fire in the corridor between their apartments.

On either side of the girl is a honeycomb of apartments. Wooden poles create the apartment framework. Each living space is twelve feet wide. A shelf, which runs the length of the longhouse, divides all the apartments into an upper and lower section. People sleep on a platform in the lower half. Below this platform, and on the shelf above, is storage space.

The girl knows she will have to help her mother with chores, but there is one chore she enjoys doing all on her own. The girl reaches under the sleeping platform and searches through the snowshoes, bows, and baskets, looking for the gourd and the wooden mallet. She cannot find it.

She carefully steps on the platform and reaches up to the storage space above her. She feels about between skin robes and baskets of food. There it is! It is just as she thought, her older brother had hidden the gourd and mallet from her.

She grabs them and dashes outside, passing the family crest of the turtle painted above the door. She runs through her village, passing women bringing back water from the river. The girl approaches the towering fence of straight tree trunks. She doesn't care that this wooden wall protects the village from attack. At the moment it is merely an obstacle between her and her destination: the cornfield.

She passes through the fence entrance toward the closest field. She is not the first to arrive. Crows, squirrels, rabbits, and deer are busy helping themselves to tender young ears of corn.

The girl jumps onto a wooden platform and bangs the mallet against the gourd to frighten the birds and animals away. Her brothers arrive, along with other boys, holding their bows and arrows. They yell and run as fast as they can through the cornstalks. They jump over pumpkins and between the rows of squash.

The crows scatter. Deer bolt through the field, bending cornstalks and making a loud, rustling sound.

The boys leave the field. They stand before the woods. This is their world. No woman can hunt, trade, or go to war. In, and beyond, these woods is where they will spend most of their lives.

They move through the forest, quietly, with bows in hand and arrows in pouches. Today could be the day. If any of the boys kill a deer, they can leave the world of play and hunt with the men.

The girl stops banging on the gourd. She looks out on the cornfield glowing in the morning sunshine. The boys in the woods stop. In the distance a deer is nibbling on some wild berries. The boys mimic the deer and nibble on the wild berries that surround them.

The girl must leave the field to help her mother. The boys must continue playing, trying to become good hunters. But they all carry the same silent wish, if only summer could last forever.

Understanding the Clan

Each clan was an extended family. The members held a single animal in honor. This animal was revered for certain qualities it possessed. The bear, in the bear clan, was honored because it was powerful, and yet a peaceful creature.

Members of the bear clan did not eat bear meat. They felt it was disrespectful. They also made the bear their totem and placed this crest on the ends of their longhouse.

Each longhouse was occupied by families belonging to the same clan. The eldest woman was the leader of the longhouse. Today, the Iroquois still honor their clans. At Iroquois gatherings people commonly ask, "What is your clan?"

The boys move through the forest quietly.

Eating Off the Land

Iroquois families ate only when they were hungry. If there was one main meal of the day it was usually in the morning. Depending on the season, meals included deer meat, fresh and smoked fish, such as bluefish and trout, and vegetables. Women made a variety of squash and corn dishes. Food was flavored with maple syrup, berries, and nuts. For snacks, people ate sunflower and pumpkin seeds, and maple syrup and maple sugar candy.

THE LIFE OF THE *THREE SISTERS*

The *three sisters* were inside the longhouse. Who were these sisters? The Iroquois name for corn, bean, and squash seeds was the *three sisters*.

The *three sisters* had been inside all winter. They wanted to return to the earth. They could not, not yet. The ground wasn't yet ready for them. The earth was cold and wet. If the *three sisters* were to return now, they would rot and die.

When would the earth be ready? The oak leaves had the answer. When they were the size of a red squirrel's foot, then the ground would be safe for the *three sisters*.

The men made digging sticks and sharpened old ones needed for planting. They cleared fields by burning unwanted trees and weeds un-der the women's supervision. The women soaked *sisters* in medicine. Crows hated this medicine. When the *three sisters* were planted, the crows wouldn't steal them from the ground.

The ground got warmer and drier as the days got longer. The oak leaves continued to grow. In late May, the leaves said it was time to plant, for the *three sisters* to leave the longhouse. Older people blessed them before their journey back to the earth.

Hunched over, the women walked the fields digging up hills of earth with their sticks, and placing each *sister*—corn, bean, and squash—into the sun-warmed ground.

By summer, the land was crowded with young crops. Animals came to eat the sweet vegetables. The *three sisters* needed protection. The children chased the animals and birds away.

They hung the ears inside the longhouse to be dried for food and seed.

The beans were first to ripen. Women picked, shelled, and stored them in baskets. Some would be for food, some would be seeds for planting. Then women picked the squash, cut the flesh into strips, and dried it on roofs and on the ground. The seeds in the squash were also dried. A portion of these seeds would also be used for planting.

The corn was harvested last, when the weather was cold. Both men and women joined in. They talked and laughed as they snapped off ears of corn in the husks. They hung the ears inside the longhouse to be dried for food and seed. Below the hanging corn were baskets of bean and squash seeds. Once again, the *three sisters* were together.

Dried Corn Soup

Fresh corn soup was a treat. For most of the year the people had soup made from dried corn. Below is a recipe for dried corn soup.

1 cup of crushed dried corn, or ready-made cornmeal
4 cups of water
animal fat or maple sugar for seasoning (optional)

If you are using dried corn, the corn has to be pounded into a meal. Place the kernels in a bowl and crush them with a palm-size stone till they have turned into a powder. Pour 3 cups of water into a large saucepan and bring the water to a boil.

Mix the remaining cup of cold water with the cornmeal in the bowl. Add the cornmeal mixture to the boiling water.

Turn down the heat to simmer. Stir the soup occasionally. When the soup gets somewhat thick, it is ready to eat. Add bacon fat or maple sugar to season the soup. You can also add butter and salt, to taste. It's simple, but satisfying.

The Big Heads

The messengers walk through the village.

The messengers walk through the snow-covered village. They are wearing snowshoes and buffalo robes that are tied around their heads with braids of cornhusks.

"It's our uncles. It's the Big Heads," shout the children as the messengers enter the long-houses to stir the fireplace ashes with their paddles. The children knew they were coming. They come every year.

The old year has ended. The appearance of the *Big Heads* in late January or early February marks the beginning of the new year. It is also the start of the five-day Midwinter Festival.

On the first day of the festival a white dog is killed, then decorated with red paint and white wampum, and hung from a pole. This dog represents purity and will be the village's messenger to the Creator at the end of the festival.

The next morning the ashes are stirred again, this time by spiritual leaders and then ordinary people. People sing songs of thanks and perform dances to awaken past dreams. Dreams are all important to the people. A person's dreams tell what his soul needs to remain strong. Only if the soul gets what it desires will a person have good fortune in life. The Midwin-

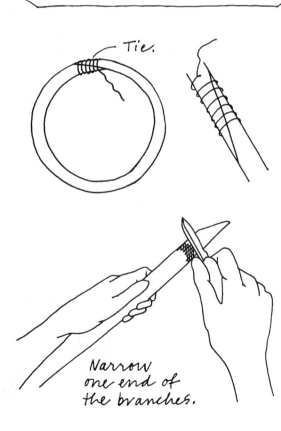

Tie.

Narrow one end of the branches.

Seneca Hoop-and-Pole Game

The Hoop-and-Pole Game was played by Indians throughout North America. The Seneca played the game with a hoop and javelin, 5 to 6 feet long. Two sides lined up in rows. Each person on a side held three to six javelins. If a player hit the rolling hoop, the player kept the javelin. If the player missed, the javelin was given to the opposing side. The first side to have all the javelins wins. Here's a version of the Hoop-and-Pole Game you can play.

You Will Need:

An adult to help you, ten hardwood sticks, one sapling or pliable branch, a pocketknife, strong string or twine, and a flat, outdoor surface.

1. Have an adult help you trim both ends of your branch or sapling on an angle, as shown at left. Soak it in water overnight. It will now be more flexible, and you can bend it into a circle with an 8-inch diameter. Tie the ends with strong string or twine so the angles join together.

2. Take one of your ten branches and, with the help of the adult, narrow one end of the branch. It doesn't have to be narrowed to a point. Do the same with the other branches.

Now decide who rolls the hoop first, how far away the person rolling the hoop stands from the javelin thrower, and how fast the hoop is to be rolled.

For example, you may decide 10 feet is an acceptable distance. The javelin thrower must stand 10 feet away from the hoop roller, but the javelin thrower can throw the javelin from any position behind this imaginary line.

The Seneca chose managers to make decisions about distance and the speed of the hoop based on the skill of the players. You should do the same.

Now each player takes five javelins. The hoop roller rolls the hoop. The player throws a javelin. If the javelin misses the hoop, the player gives up the javelin to the opponent. Now it's the opponent's turn. The first time a person hits the hoop, he or she sets the spot from which every javelin must be thrown. The players continue to take turns until one person has all the javelins. That player is the winner.

ter Festival invites people to remember their dreams.

One man remembers a dream he had when a terrible pain invaded his arms and legs. In the dream he saw one of the False Faces, or magical masks, worn by members of the False Face Society. This society's purpose is to cure sickness.

He called on the False Face Society to come to his house and cure his pain. The society honored his request. They danced around him in his longhouse. Not long after, the pain left his arms and legs.

Every year at the Midwinter Festival he asks the society to return to his house to dance and honor his past dream. By doing this he hopes to keep his pain away for another year. The False Face Society dances in his house as well as in the other village longhouses. Other curing societies are also called upon to visit people's homes. The village is alive with dances.

A woman remembers dreaming about the Great Riddle Ceremony. The village renews her old dream. Everyone who has had a dream during the past year walks from house to house, giving hints to other people about their dreams in the form of riddles. The listener has to guess what the dreamer's dream is about. If the listener's guess is right, the person has to satisfy the wish of the dreamer's dream.

A man who had a dream just two months ago enters a longhouse and states his riddle to a woman: "I am looking for the lonely sister." The woman thinks for a moment. She realizes that since corn is the last of the *three sisters* to be harvested, the man must be seeking corn.

She gives the man dried ears of corn. They both are relieved. If she hadn't had any corn to give the man his dream wouldn't have been satisfied. An unsatisfied dream can bring the dreamer misfortune.

The third day arrives, finally! It is the day the children have been waiting for. Boys and girls crowd around a woman elder. Together they wander through the village asking for presents of tobacco. If a person doesn't give them tobacco, or some present, the children are free to steal as much of the person's possessions as they can get away with.

Through the snow they wander, laughing, searching for people to stop. They spot a man going into the longhouse. They stop him and ask for tobacco. The man doesn't have any tobacco.

The man rushes inside. The children rush after him. They plunder his apartment and scurry outside, carrying baskets of beans, skins, and food. One boy found a dish of maple sugar pieces. The other children swarm around him for pieces of the candy.

On the fourth day, the village chief asks that the dances end and everyone gather in the council longhouse. There, the various societies perform the dances they are known for. The Corn Husk Society members dress in women's clothing, for women represent the earth and all that she provides. They dance in a circular pattern, stomping their feet and shaking rattles. The Bear Society performs their dance. They waddle and shuffle their feet. Members of the False Face Society act as clowns.

The final day has arrived. The dances and the games are now just memories. The spiritual leaders remove the dog from its pole, and burn the animal. The dog's spirit is free. Its spirit travels up to the Creator and offers the village's thanks for the blessings given to them over the last year. Another year is over. A new year and new dreams have begun.

The man rushes inside. The children rush after him.

Winter Games

The sticks quivered over the icy track.

The Bowl Game

During the Midwinter Festival Iroquois men played the Bowl Game. In a wooden bowl men placed six peach pits. One side of each pit had been burnt black. The other side was painted white.

Teams were formed. One player from a team banged the bowl against the ground. If five or six pits turned up the same color, his team scored and the player continued. If not, the bowl was handed to the other team.

You can play this game. All you need is a pie pan or shallow bowl and six fruit pits or dried beans. Paint one side of the beans, or pits, black. Paint the other side white. You're ready to play!

Snowsnakes

Snowsnakes was a popular snow sport played by many Indians in North America, including the Iroquois. For the Iroquois, the object of the game was to see who could throw a stick farthest down a long trough made in the snow. Sounds simple. It was not.

First, someone had to make the stick. It took skill to turn an ordinary hickory or maple branch into a sleek rod that could travel over icy surfaces at tremendous speeds.

The sticks were 5 to 9 feet long, and an inch wide at the stick's head, narrowing to less than ½ inch at the end. Most of the stick was ¼ inch thick. The stick's tip was cone-shaped and weighted with lead.

For the trough, a smooth log was dragged through the snow over and over to create a trough that was 1,500 feet long and over a foot deep! Water was poured into the trough. The water froze, creating a smooth, slick surface.

At the game, individuals or groups could compete. As each person, or group, waited their turn, "doctors" treated the sticks with beeswax and animal oils. This helped the stick race more smoothly over the surface, which meant the stick would travel farther.

If two teams were playing, each player launched his stick down the trough. The sticks looked like snakes as they quivered over the icy track.

When everyone had their turn, the side whose snowsnake had traveled the farthest distance received a point. If the snowsnakes of the second- and third-place finishers also belonged to the winning side, they received an additional two points. The game continued until one side reached the agreed upon total number of points. The winning team won whatever the two teams had wagered.

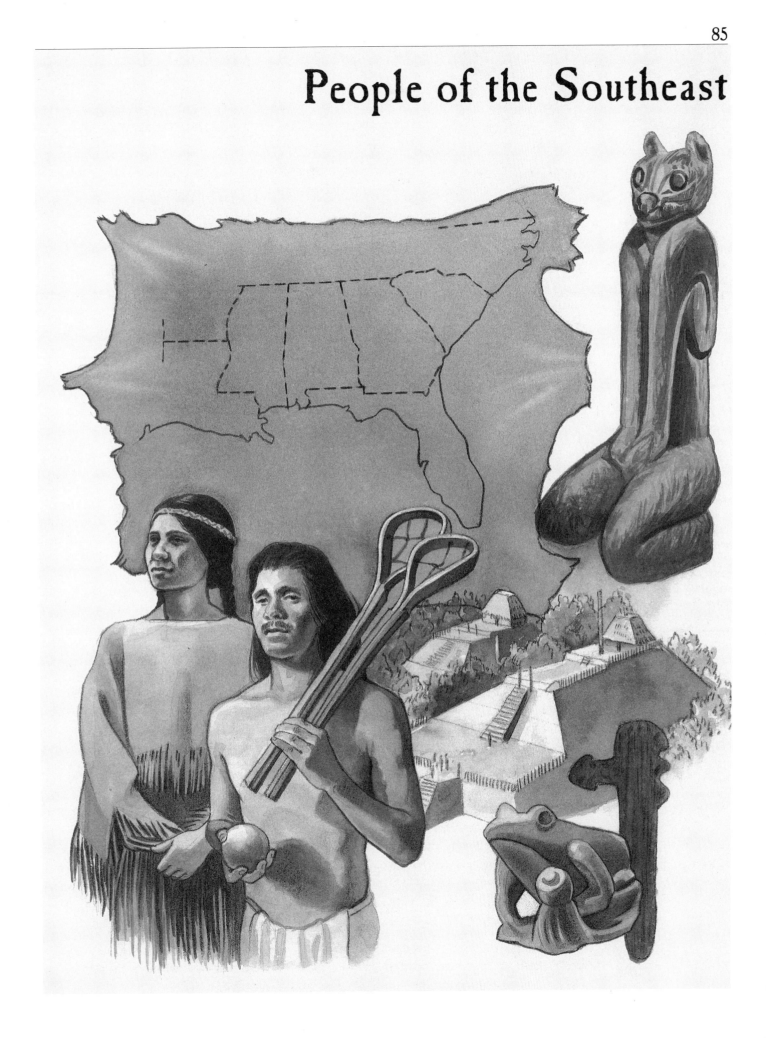

People of the Southeast

The Mounds of Cahokia

The chief gazed out from his home atop a towering mound of earth. Before him was the city Cahokia with its broad plaza surrounded by many villages.

It was early morning. All across the flat, green land many of the thirty thousand residents had started fires in their homes. The smoke rose up through their dried grass roofs, creating miles of white ribbons in the sky.

By the only entrance to the city, traders, their paid bearers, and city workers lined up waiting to be let in. A guard questioned each person before allowing him to pass through the small gate shaped like an "L." The city designers created the gate this way to prevent large groups of people from rushing the guard and entering the city.

The wait was long. For those who had traveled to the city by canoe on Cahokia Creek, the wait was an annoyance, a test of their patience. For the bearers paid to carry a trader's supply of stone, it was a test of their strength. These men would get no rest till they reached the city marketplace.

One bearer was not thinking about the dark flintlike rocks he was carrying. He was thinking about Cahokia. As a boy, he had watched the daily departure of farmers and traders to take their products to the city behind the walls. He had pestered the men, on their return, to tell him of Cahokia. He begged them to hire him as a bearer. They laughed and told him to stop asking and keep growing. He would see Cahokia in time. Now it was his time.

Passing through the gate, the bearer desperately wanted to stop and look around. He had no choice but to follow his trader. The bearer noticed mounds everywhere. He walked by open courts where children played. He passed hundreds of bare-backed men who were carrying baskets of dirt between villages. The bearer saw, among the clay and pole houses of the villages, that certain homes stood above the others upon high mounds.

These are the homes of the wealthy, he thought; the higher the mound the wealthier the person. He kept moving. Once again, he observed men who carried baskets of dirt.

The bearer stopped, even though his body ached to remove the enormous weight he was carrying. He couldn't believe the size of the mound he was standing next to. He squinted his eyes as he looked up, trying to see the flattened summit 100 feet from the ground. All of Cahokia lived in this mound's shadow. It was the chief's mound, which was 700 feet wide and 1,000 feet long.

The bearer again saw bare men who were carrying baskets of dirt. This time, though, he spotted them dumping the dirt from their baskets onto the ground. A new mound was being formed.

He realized what he had heard was true. These mounds were not created by nature. Workers, hired by the wealthy, carried basket after basket of dirt to form the earthworks. He wondered how long it would take to complete the mound. He had no idea that many of the men who were carrying dirt would never live to see the mound completed. The chief's mound took over two hundred years to build.

A Society Comes and Goes

The city of Cahokia was part of a larger civilization that stretched from what is now the southeast of the United States, to Oklahoma in the west, and Wisconsin to the north. This society was called the Mississippian Society. It began in A.D. 800.

Cahokia was located near where the Illinois town of East St. Louis is today. Around A.D. 1200 the city declined. The reason is not clear.

Some experts believe the people of Cahokia moved to other nearby cities. Others believe Cahokia became so large it became impossible to grow enough food to feed the city's people. Whatever the reason, the great city of Cahokia was eventually abandoned.

The bearer raced to catch up with his trader. Fortunately, the trader hadn't noticed the bearer had been lagging behind. The trader entered the bright, open plaza. It was a maze of traders and craftsmen, all urging the passersby to see their wares that rested beside them on the ground.

The bearer's employer maneuvered his way through the crowd, talking to potential buyers. Craftsmen, who were making arrowheads, baskets, and pottery, discussed business with wealthy men who wanted to buy their goods and sell them many miles away. A jeweler argued with a customer over the worth of his fresh-pearl jewelry.

The trader stopped. He ordered the bearer to put down his merchandise. The bearer released his heavy burden and looked out beyond the people-filled plaza at the burial mounds, and the mounds that held temples. The mounds mesmerized him. Someday, he pondered, I will live in Cahokia, even if I have to carry baskets of dirt.

The plaza was a maze of traders and craftsmen.

A CHEROKEE BALL GAME

Cypress, white pine, and ash trees cover the round, rolling hills known as the Appalachian highlands. Clouds gather and wander between the hills, through the trees. This year's corn has been picked in the Cherokee village. There is food for winter. It is the perfect time to play the racket ball game *Istapoli*, also called Lacrosse.

A messenger from one village was sent to one nearby to issue a challenge to a game of *Istapoli*. He carried painted sticks adorned with ribbons. A man from the village touched the sticks. The challenge was accepted.

The men train. They tumble, run, and pass the wooden ball between them, catching it in the loose webbing of their hickory sticks. The sticks look like large spoons, the spoon portions made up of loosely connected strings or twisted squirrel skin.

The players are purified. The shaman takes them to the water's edge to take part in a ritual called "goes to water." He readies each player for victory.

The next day, in both villages, they hold a ball-play dance. The men dance to the shaking of the rattle, held by another man who circles the players. The women stand in a line. They move toward the men, then wheel and turn away from them, to the beat of the drum and the constant chanting. When the women dancers are tired, other women take their place. The men are not allowed replacements.

It is night. The dancing continues. The drumming continues. The chanting continues. The *talala*, a person who has mastered a frightening yell, leaves the dance. He goes off toward the opponent's village. He lets out four yells that sound like a woodpecker rapping on a dead tree. The opponents' village hears these yells.

It is hoped these sounds will terrify their opponents so much they will not want to play. The *talala* comes back and says, "They are already beaten." In the distance, the *talala* from the opponents' village can be heard. Both sides proclaim they will win.

It is sunrise. The players take their sticks and follow their shaman to the playing field, located between the two competing villages. Along the way, the shaman from each village will stop the players four times to perform the "go to water" ritual with each player. As a player is taken by the shaman, the others talk about the upcoming game and work on their sticks.

After the fourth stop the shaman speaks to the men. The shaman praises his players. He talks only of victory.

One team reaches the playing field; the *talala* comes forward and once again lets out his frightening yell. The shaman takes the men by the water. He marks off a portion of the ground to represent the playing field. He takes a small bundle of sharp sticks in his hand and uses them to show the players where to position themselves on the field.

The players are scratched by the shaman with

The Cross Within a Circle

The Cherokee people believed, as did other peoples in the Southeast, that there were three levels of sky: the Upper, Middle, and Lower Worlds. Each was connected by four cords. There was a cord tied in the north, south, east, and west.

On This World, two lines were drawn to connect the four cords. These two lines divided This World, which was a circle, into four sections. Or, to see it another way, it was a cross within a circle. The people saw the cross within a circle as a symbol of the human world.

Each section in this circle was connected to color. Each color had a meaning. North was the direction of cold. This section was blue. It represented trouble or defeat. South was in the direction of warmth. Its color was white. It represented peace and happiness. The east was the color red. This was the direction from which the sun rose. It was also the color of blood. Red represented life and success. West was black. It was where the moon set. It had no warmth. It was where death lived.

He carried painted sticks adorned with ribbons.

The two teams run toward each other, shouting.

a comb of turkey bone splinters. The scratches are painful. But they believe it will guarantee their victory.

The team returns to the field. The challenging players have yet to arrive. The men decorate their bodies with paints. They place hawk and eagle feathers in their hair. They attach squirrel and bat hair, and parts of bat wings to their sticks. The players believe they will be as swift and precise in defeating their enemy as the bat, the hawk, and the eagle.

The challenging team enters the field yelling. The other team answers with their own yells. The people from both villages have gathered around the playing field. It is level and about 230 feet long. Twenty-foot-high goalposts are standing on either end.

The two teams come to the center of the field. Today there are ten players on each side. They are barefoot and wear cloths around their waists. Each player is holding a pair of sticks.

Men and women, from both villages, wager articles they have brought. The villages bet everything they have. There is no fear of losing. The people know that they can replace everything lost here today.

It is time to play. The two teams take their positions at opposite ends of the field. An old man, holding the ball, tells both sides to behave as their fathers before them have done. He warns them to hold their tempers. The two teams run toward each other from opposite ends of the field, shouting. The old man throws the ball onto the field. The game begins.

Players from both teams race around the field, kicking, tripping, stamping on, and tackling their opponents, in an attempt to find, as much get, the ball.

A player from the challenging team scoops up the ball into one of his webbed sticks. He can either run or pass the ball to a teammate. The player decides to run. He throws the ball to a teammate, but it is intercepted by a player from the other team. The players quickly change direction.

The team with the ball runs and passes their way toward their opponents' goal. A player shoots and scores. But it will not be the last score of the game. There will many others until one team has twelve goals. The winning village will take all the articles that have been wagered. They will also take with them the belief that the rituals performed before the game are as important as the game itself.

Forbidden Foods

One week to twenty-eight days before a game of *Istapoli*, players were not allowed to eat certain foods that lacked the qualities that a player needed to win. No player could eat rabbit, because it was a shy, anxious animal. They were not able to eat frog, because its bones were easily destroyed. The players also couldn't eat any young animals, or touch any infants, because they were weak. Hog-sucker fish were also forbidden, because they were slow moving.

Players ate only those foods that were known to be strong and cunning. The raccoon, with its ability to be fierce and shrewd when under attack, made a fitting food.

A Cherokee Legend

It was believed that once long ago, the animals challenged the birds to a game of racket ball. Wagers and rules were made. The animals took their positions on the ground.

There was the bear, with his large weight, the deer who could run fast, and the terrapin (a fresh-water turtle) who could withstand harsh blows.

The birds stood in the trees. There was the eagle, the hawk, and the magic bird, the Great Hawk Tlaniwa. They were all very quick and strong flyers.

The birds waited for the ball to be thrown up to them. All of a sudden, up the tree came two tiny animals. They asked the bird captain if they could join the birds' side and play.

The birds laughed. They asked why they hadn't joined the animals. The creatures said they had, but the animals said they were too small.

The bird captain felt sorry for them and allowed them to join their side. But there was a problem. They couldn't fly. The birds held a discussion and came up with a plan.

They swooped down and cut off pieces of the leather from the drum on the ground and attached them to the legs of one of the tiny animals. They had created Tlameha, the bat.

Up came the ball. The bat surrounded the ball and kept it afloat with its wings, not allowing the ball to drop to the ground.

The birds realized that the same thing must be done to the other creature. But there was no leather left on the drum. There was only one solution, to use the tiny animal's own skin.

Two birds stood on either side of the creature and began to pull and pull. When they were done they had created the Tewa, the flying squirrel.

The bird captain tested the flying squirrel. The ball was thrown in the air. The flying squirrel caught the ball and raced through the air to another tree a hundred feet away. The birds' team was ready.

The game began. The flying squirrel caught the ball and tossed it to the other birds, who kept it in the air and out of the animals' reach.

Eventually, the ball fell toward the ground. It was just about within the animals' reach when the bat grabbed it—swerving and dodging the animals' attempts to get the ball.

The bat threw the ball at the animals' goal and scored. The birds won the game. To this day, players plead to the bat and the flying squirrel to give them their power of swiftness and precision.

Playing Chunkey

In many villages throughout the Southeast, the people played Chunkey. The Chunkey field, which was also used to perform ceremonies, dominated the village with its length of about 200 feet. Sometimes the field was sunk several feet into the earth.

In playing Chunkey, two men each held a pole about 8 feet long. One player held a Chunkey stone. This stone was wheel-shaped, carefully polished, and was owned by the village or clan.

The player with the stone rolled it across the field. The two players ran several yards and then threw their poles where they thought the stone was going to land.

The Cherokee allowed points to be scored based on how close the stone came to certain marks made on the pole. Other Indian groups scored by giving two points to the player whose pole was close to the stone. If neither player's pole was very close, the closest one received one point. The game was played until a player reached twelve points.

You too can play Chunkey. You will need a large open area, fairly flat and free of grass, two 4-foot branches, and a rounded stone, or a ball. Score two points for the pole that is very close to the stone, or one point for the closer of the two poles.

Chunkey yard

Chunkey stone

The Alligator Hunt

The watchman quickly called out for assistance.

The sun was rising. A Timucua man sat in a narrow house watching the River of the Deer, the Suwannee, for alligators. Alligators often came onto land when they were hungry. And when they did, the watchman had to be ready to warn the village.

The watchman slapped at a mosquito. He looked out through a large crack in the wall and onto the cypress trees draped with moss. Suddenly, several wild turkeys raced by the watchman's house. Anxiously, he searched the dark water for an approaching alligator.

Back at the village, boys were already outside pretending to hunt alligators, in anticipation. It wasn't certain that an alligator would appear today, but the people knew the animal's habits. The entire village felt the alligators would appear.

Women worked outside gathering wood for the fire that would smoke the alligators' meat. The men came out of the sweathouse. They had purified themselves and honored the alligator, who was going to allow itself to be killed for food. The men now attended to working on their hunting weapons.

At the river, the man continued his watch. If an alligator came ashore unannounced, he would be punished. It was not easy to watch. The man yawned, and as he did the water rippled and an alligator poked his head out of the river. In a moment he was on the shore.

The alligator announced his arrival with a loud bellow. The watchman quickly called out for assistance as he stepped outside and grabbed the pole leaning against the watch house. The alligator moved toward the village searching for food. The man followed.

In the village, the hunters grabbed their

weapons and passed through a narrow gate, past the protective fence and the guards. Dogs barked with excitement. Boys were eager to join in the hunt, but they were not old enough.

The hunters came upon the alligator. The alligator opened its jaws. As it did several hunters shoved a long pole down its throat. This made the alligator's dangerous jaws useless.

Watching out for the alligator's tail, the hunters turned it over on its back and attacked the alligator's soft belly with clubs and spears. When the alligator was dead, it was brought back to the village. There it would be gutted and smoked on a raised wooden rack.

Another man went down to the river to take over the watch. Perhaps other alligators would come onto shore today. The day had just begun.

Hit the Target, Then Eat

Boys began their training to be skillful hunters at an early age. This was true for Indian peoples throughout North America. When Powhatan boys got up in the morning, they took their bows and arrows and practiced shooting moss or sticks that were thrown into the air.

No boy could eat until he hit his target.

The hunters came upon the alligator.

The Great Canoe

She saw a strange shape floating in the distance.

"Where We Came Together"

The Powhatan people grew tobacco. They, as other Indian groups, did not smoke tobacco daily. To do so would have been considered disrespectful. Tobacco was sacred and was used in ceremonies to promote peace and friendship.

In the Southeast there was a legend about tobacco. A man and a woman fell in love in the woods. Sometime later, when out hunting, the man came upon the spot where he fell in love with is wife-to-be. There he found a strange plant.

This plant was brought back to the village, dried, and smoked. It was named "Where We Came Together." The elders stated that since the man and the woman were so calm and joyous when tobacco was created, it should be smoked to promote peace and friendship.

Now was the time! The river was low. A group of Powhatan boys began making a bridge out of pine branches. Others searched the muddy banks for oysters and mussels. Though the boys could not see the ocean, its influence was clearly felt. The salty ocean water that traveled up and mixed with the fresh river water had retreated with the ebbing tide.

In the village, women and girls worked in the gardens, made clay pots, and repaired clothing made of deer hide. The men were not in the village; they were fishing in the bay. Nearby, smoke rose into the clear sky. Fish was being roasted. The boys stopped playing. They raced through the pine and oak woods. They passed through the village and kept on going. The girls joined them.

The children jumped off a small hill onto the beach. They ran toward the men who were roasting fish over wooden racks. A man came up to the fire and emptied his basket of fish. The children looked for a moment at the fish jumping about; some had bone hooks stuck in their mouths. All eyes turned to the roasting fish.

One of them was ready. The man placed it before the children on some sticks. They let it cool, then they enjoyed their feast. There was no need to worry about saving some for later. The ocean provided all the fish they could eat.

When the children were full, they ran across the beach chasing sand crabs. They stopped to look for clams. Finding nothing, they ran off again. One girl stopped. She didn't feel like playing. She sat down and looked out at the bay, toward the ocean beyond.

She saw a strange shape floating in the far distance. She tried to determine what it was. She knew she had never seen anything like it before. It was a white shape that seemed to float on the water. As she watched, it came closer. The girl ran to the men at the fire and told them what she had seen. Soon everyone was at the edge of the water watching the strange white thing come slowly closer. As they watched, the men realized that there was a dark shape under the white one. It looked like a canoe. But it was the largest canoe they had ever seen. The white shape was its sail. What spirit had sent this great canoe to them?

If You Want to Know More

The things you've learned in this book about American Indians can be the start of your journey to other discoveries. This section lists resources—books, videos, activities, and cultural places—that will tell you more about the things you like best.

Books

You can find other books about Indian lifeways that interest you. Use the subject section of your library's card file or computer or ask the reference librarian to suggest books written by and about American Indians.

Do you know how handmade rafts and canoes once carried people across rivers and oceans? *California Indian Watercraft*, by Richard Cunningham (EZ Nature Books, 1989) will steer you through the building secrets of California tribes, with examples of their watercraft.

You can get the facts about rediscovering the Makah Indian village at Ozette, Washington, in *Hunters of the Whale: An Adventure in Northwest Coast Archaeology*, by Ruth Kirk, with Richard D. Daugherty (William Morrow and Company, Inc., 1974). It tells how the village was excavated, what they found, and the careful digging that student archaeologists and Indians did to protect their discoveries.

Are you looking for more good Indian legends and stories? The elders of the Lenape group told their people about the first snowfall, a storm that threatened to bury all the animals. Was there no one who could save them? Find *Rainbow Crow*, a Lenape tale retold by Nancy Van Laan (Dragonfly Books, 1989) and you'll know what the Lenape know.

Paul Goble has written several award-winning children's books about the lives of Indians in the days long before you were born. He's an artist, too, who tells of people facing adventure and trouble. You'll read quickly to see what happens to a child on the Plains in *The Girl Who Loved Wild Horses* (Macmillan Children's Book Group, 1986). *Death of the Iron Horse* (Macmillan Children's Book Group, 1993) is a true story about the Cheyenne people and the railroad.

If you appreciate the special ways that grandparents teach kids, *Seya's Song*, by Ron Hirschi (Sasquatch Books, 1992), is just the book for you. In it, you'll meet a young S'Klallam village girl, find out what her life was like, and discover what she learned from her grandmother.

Activities

Have you played all the games in this book and wish there were more? *Games of the North American Indians*, by Stewart Culin (Dover Publications, 1975), will keep you busy. It's written for adults, but don't let that stop you. The book is organized by kinds of games. Start by challenging your favorite grown-up to the Zuni stick game (page 266), and then let him or her choose a game and challenge *you*.

Maybe you'd like to make an insect habitat or start a craft project. *Keepers of the Earth* and *Keepers of the Animals*, by Michael Caduto and Joseph Bruchac (Fulcrum Publishing, 1989, 1991), and *Indian Picture Writing*, by Robert Hofsinde (William Morrow and Company, 1959), are packed with activities and crafts to make.

If you're hungry for Indian food, you need *Spirit of the Harvest*, by Cox and Davis (Stewart, Tabori, and Chang, 1991). But it's filled with more than recipes. Along with beautiful photographs of Indian artwork and objects, its bold Indian designs will give you ideas for decorating your own projects.

Videos

There are plenty of videos and movies about American Indians that you can rent. But it's not so easy to find the ones that portray Native Americans realistically. Your video store should have *Dances with Wolves*, starring Kevin Costner. It will give you a pretty accurate and realistic idea of the life of the Plains Indians during the late nineteenth century, when the people were driven off their homelands. Have you heard Indians speak their own languages? You can. Rent *Windwalker*, a movie about a baby twin boy taken from his tribe by enemies. Nearly everyone in the cast is Indian, and they speak only Cheyenne and Crow, with English subtitles.

Tribal Lands and Cultural Sites

Throughout the U.S., private tribal lands, historic sites, and museums can teach you about Indian cultures as they were and are. A few are described here, to give you an idea about places to visit when you travel. Ask your librarian to help you find the names of Indian cultural centers close to your home.

If you're traveling to another state, write to the state capital, in care of the Department of Tourism, and ask for a list of places where you can visit Native Americans and attend public Indian events during the year. Also check the resource lists at the back of *America's Fascinating Indian Heritage* (Reader's Digest Books, 1978).

Did you know you can camp on many Indian reservations in the United States? Be sure to obey the rules, just as you would at any campground. You might meet Indian kids your own age, get to watch ceremonies or festivals, or even try some Indian food. For the names and addresses of these reservations, write to the Bureau of Indian Affairs, U.S. Department of the Interior, Washington, D.C. 20245. List the states you are interested in and ask for information about camping facilities and events you can attend.

On the Road

The Anasazi Indians may have been the first people to see the Grand Canyon. You can explore the remains of a small Anasazi settlement east of Grand Canyon Village in northern Arizona. From Grand Canyon Village, drive twenty-seven miles east on East Rim Drive to Tusayan Museum. The museum holds models showing Anasazi homes eight hundred years ago. A trail from the museum leads to the village remains, where thirty people once lived.

Three hours east of the Grand Canyon, by car, is Canyon de Chelly (de-SHAY), another old Anasazi settlement. About A.D. 1, the Anasazi spent winters in caves in the canyon. In the summer they made homes of poles and brush. Over the next hundreds of years they built stone houses in the cliffs above the canyon floor. We think about a thousand people once lived in the cluster of villages in Canyon de Chelly.

Today the canyon is part of Navajo reservation land and Navajo families still live and farm here. You can drive along a scenic canyon rim road and you can hike a trail to White House Ruin. All other areas are off limits, unless you have an approved guide. Without disturbing the privacy of canyon residents, the guide can show you some ancient and fascinating ruins.

South of Phoenix, Arizona, is Arizona's largest prehistoric Indian site, Casa Grande Ruins National Monument. Its Spanish name, *Casa Grande*, means "big house." Hohokam (HO-HO-kam) Indians built it about seven hundred years ago. The largest building is four stories tall, with eleven rooms, and its walls are between two and four feet thick. (To protect it from damaging weather, a huge "roof" now covers it.) Inside the visitors center, glass-case displays explain what life was like in this valley hundreds of years ago. The Hohokam pottery, baskets, dishes, and tools in the center show the objects they made here, before they left Casa Grande—no one knows why—in about A.D. 1450.

A few miles north of San Francisco, California, visit the Fall Acorn Festival or the Spring Strawberry Festival at Kule Loklo Miwok Indian Village, Point Reyes National Seashore, Inverness, California 94937. Miwok and Pomo tour guides will tell you about the reconstructed village, and you may have the opportunity to hear Indian songs and stories.

Stand in the central plaza at Cahokia Mounds State Historic Park, in Collinsville, Illinois, and you're in the largest archaeological site in the United States—over two thousand acres total! Sixty-eight earth mounds still tower above the land. Monks Mound is a thousand feet tall and spans over fourteen acres. West of Monks Mound is Woodhenge, an ancient calendar. It is made of forty-eight posts set within a circle 410 feet wide. At 5:10 A.M. on June 22, you can meet to celebrate the Summer Solstice. Set your alarm clock! During the rest of the year, too, there is a lot to do at Cahokia Mounds, including crafts classes, games, arrowhead-making, and spear-throwing. The Heritage Special America Event is held in late September. The site comes alive with activities like storytelling, ceremonial dancing, and demonstrations. For details, write to Cahokia Mounds State Historic Site, Box 382, Collinsville, IL 62234, (618) 346-5160.

Iroquois life is explained at the Schoharie Museum of the Iroquois Indians, Box 158, Schoharie, New York 12157, (518) 295-8553, or (518) 234-2276. The museum has both ancient and modern displays of Iroquois life. During Labor Day weekend, the State University of New York, in Cobleskill, presents a public festival. Write to the museum for more details.

Index